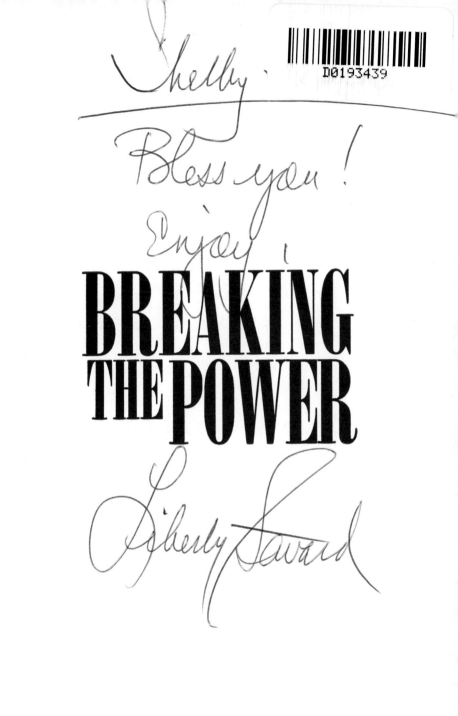

Shelby :

Bless you !

Enjoy !

BREAKING THE POWER

Liberty Savard

BREAKING THE POWER

Liberty Savard

Bridge-Logos *Publishers*

North Brunswick, NJ

Breaking The Power
by Liberty Savard
ISBN 0-88270-699-3
Library of Congress Catalog Card Number: 97-77217
Copyright ©1997 by Liberty Savard
Revised October 1997

Published by:
Bridge-Logos *Publishers*
North Brunswick Corporate Center
1300 Airport Road, Suite E
North Brunswick, NJ 08902-1700

Dedication

This book is dedicated to
my grandmother Mary Grace Miller,
who prayed and believed for my
salvation
and then saw the fruit of her prayers
come to pass.
She went home to be with the Lord in
November of 1988.

And to "SARAH,"
my cousin Susan Diane Beason,
whose life was a "hands-on" training
experience for the working out of
Shattering Your Strongholds.
"SARAH" went home to be with the
Lord in November of 1994.

My dearest Grandma and Susie,
the circle will once again be unbroken!

Table of Contents

The Bridge..ix

1. Don't Look Back For Your Destiny...................................1

2. Body, Soul, Spirit, and Strongholds................................17

3. Satanic/Soulish Deception of the Church.........................41

4. Wrong Behaviors, Word Curses, and Generational
   Bondages..65

5. Unmet Needs, Unhealed Hurts, and Unresolved Issues........93

6. Relationships and Agreements.......................................123

7. Soul Power and Soul-Ties...147

8. Now, Just Do It!...173

9. Tying Up Loose Ends..199

10. Are You Ready for Your Future?...................................221

The Bridge

These next few pages are intended to be a bridge between the original revelation on binding and loosing principles in *Shattering Your Strongholds* and the next level of the revelation, *Breaking the Power*. This revelation first began to unfold in my life in 1985, flowing out of a new understanding of Matthew 16:19 and the principles of binding and loosing.

The basic teaching on binding and loosing that I learned during my first thirteen years of Christianity involved "binding" the devil and evil spirits, while "loosing" the Holy Spirit and ministering spirits into a situation. I never did this with much assurance, because I knew there is no record of Jesus (or any of His disciples or apostles) ever binding an evil spirit or loosing the Holy Spirit or ministering spirits. When Jesus was dealing with evil spirits, He either rebuked them, silenced them, or told them to get out—sometimes all three. But Jesus did not bind evil spirits or loose the Holy Spirit or ministering spirits (angels) in any situation I have found in the Gospels.

Still, Matthew 16:19 and Matthew 18:18 clearly do tell us that Jesus said He was giving the keys of the Kingdom to His disciples, telling them, in essence,

"Whatsoever you bind/loose on earth will be bound/ loosed in heaven." I knew this spiritual principle had to mean more than the Church had yet realized. So many teachings on the keys of the Kingdom—about prayer, Word study, humility, authority in Christ, and other Christian truths—were being taught. I tried hard to put the principles of these teachings into practice in my Christian walk, but I still lacked victory in many areas of my life. I was deeply frustrated with so much personal defeat. It seemed I was always fighting, fighting, fighting Satan, but only occasionally winning little battles with this powerful enemy.

I wondered how God could have intended for us to spend our whole lives here on earth just battling with the devil for our spiritual survival. What kind of *a glorious Church without spot or wrinkle* was that? Little did I realize that this "enemy" of mine was just keeping me busy—distracted, deceived, and off-track—by allowing me to "win" so-called battles with him, believing I was making inroads into darkness. This deception kept me focused on dealing with him, which effectively kept me from getting in touch with the real troublemaker in my life—*my unsurrendered soul.*

Satan is not our real enemy. He is already a defeated foe. I know we've all heard that over and over. So, what makes anything different now? Simply that we've not known how to use the keys of the Kingdom to actually step out of our spiritual survival mentalities and onto the Rock who defeated our enemy over two thousand years ago.

This doesn't have as much to do with our level of faith as it does with our levels of scriptural understanding. As humans, we are all capable of placing intense faith in faulty understanding. This happens because even though we may be walking around with completely regenerated, born-again spirits, we are constantly in a battle with our not-yet fully restored nor transformed souls. We need to understand our internal conflict between soul and spirit to stop wasting so much time trying to resolve an unnecessary external conflict with an already defeated foe who is just a surrogate enemy! We've been spinning our "spiritual warfare" wheels for years in the Church, trying to get our lives straightened out. It's time to get better traction and get out of that mode.

So-called spiritual warfare "victories" are often just voluntary concessions from Satan to keep us in a spiritual warfare survival mode—what a diabolically clever and sneaky move on his part! It has certainly fooled a lot of Christians. If we really had to battle with Satan for our lives, he could have taken us out a long time ago. Our unsurrendered soul is our problem—not Satan, our surrogate problem. We do not have to fight Satan or his evil spirits for <u>our</u> personal victory! This entire book has been written to present you with information that will help you recognize where you are fighting fights you don't have to fight.

Loosing Attitudes of the Soul
Instead of Loosing Spirits

People often ask me how to bind and/or loose a critical spirit, a controlling spirit, a spirit of anger. Criticalness, control and manipulation, as well as anger, are <u>the attitudes of an unsurrendered soul within the individual</u>, not evil spirits that can be cast out. Casting demons and spirits out of people will never bring permanent relief when an unsurrendered soul is involved. Although deliverance is a spiritual truth, for Jesus delivered many of foul spirits, deliverance does nothing to bring an unsurrendered soul to submission. *You can't be delivered from yourself!*

Evil spirits can and do become involved when a human soul refuses to surrender to God's will and purposes for it, thereby ensuring open doors of access to wrong spiritual influences. The authority of Jesus Christ, the living Word, can be spoken into action by the Christian believer who rebukes these wrong spiritual influences and hindrances. But such deliverance is a temporary measure with few permanent and lasting effects unless the individual's unsurrendered soul's power structure is exposed and dismantled. Only then are the open doors of access closed to prevent the return of the same spiritual harassment.

There is a path to permanent freedom and wholeness that can be taken by all. This path must be taken <u>right through the middle of the stubborn resistance of the unsurrendered soul</u> which consists of a manipulative, controlling, fearful trichotomy of the mind, will, and emotions. I pray that you will follow this map, use the keys, and take that journey once and for all. The keys of binding and loosing will open every iron gate, stone wall, and stronghold that has sidetracked this journey in your life. Some have had their journey to wholeness, freedom, and spiritual power blocked for so long, they've just given up and sat down in the ashes and dirt of their pasts—hoping to hold out until Jesus comes back. You don't have to hold out any longer—you are now poised to move out!

Binding and Loosing Reviewed

The Hebrew and Greek words for "bind" and "binding" mean some very positive things—to knit, fasten, tie, weave together, wind around, and cause to coalesce and become one again—amongst other things. (See *Shattering Your Strongholds,* Chapter 4, for further information on these word studies.) The word "loose" in the Greek, *luo,* along with its companion words, *rhegnumi* and *agnumi,* means break up, destroy, dissolve, unloose, melt, put off, wreck, crack to sunder by separation of the parts, shatter into minute fragments, disrupt, lacerate, convulse with spasms, break forth, burst, rend, and tear. (See *Shattering Your Strongholds,* Chapter 5, for further understanding of these word studies.)

"Well, mercy!" was about all I could think of to say when I discovered those definitions. How wimpy we have been, particularly in our use of this word *loose.* Loose is a powerful word that can wreak spiritual terrorism on evil spirits and perform radical surgery on the unsurrendered soul. It is a word that can blow away every stronghold, vain imagination, and high thing (2 Cor. 10:4-5) that tries to exalt itself between believers and a full knowledge of their loving God and His ways!

Jesus Keeps It Simple

Our minds, wills, and emotions have faithfully squirreled away all of the personal details of our past traumas (complete with wrong beliefs and mind-sets) which are the sources of the unmet needs, unresolved issues, and unhealed hurts of our lives. These past traumas are still so real to some of us that we lose all perspective of the fact that they hurt today <u>only because they have been faithfully stored in our minds' record-keeping system</u>: the memory. Our memories are the only source of remaining power these past traumas have.

Contrary to all the conventional wisdom in the world today, it is non-productive, even dangerous, to give in to the unsurrendered soul's insistence that it must be a controlling factor in the healing of our memories. The unsurrendered soul has a hidden agenda that disrupts any flow of God's healing power. Why? Because the unsurrendered soul's control in our lives is based upon its power to retrieve the fear, pain, and humiliation from our past experiences. Christians who have never known how to get their strongholds and walls down so that God can heal their deepest needs, hurts, and issues live fearfully within the constraints of their souls' ability to bring traumatic memories to the surface of their minds.

The church world of the last half of this century has tried so many theories, doctrines, and programs in its attempts to bring healing and freedom to believers. And all along, as so much of the good news of the Gospel of Jesus Christ continues to prove itself to be, the answer has been simple. Jesus Christ always kept things simple. He never wanted those who trusted in Him to be dependent upon anything other than the Word and His loving, healing, strengthening design for their lives. He never wanted His lambs to be dependent upon counselors, programs, groups, etc., although each such entity may have a <u>temporary place</u> in their overcoming.

Jesus said that He was giving the keys of the Kingdom to the Church and that whatsoever believers would bind/loose on earth was bound/loosed in heaven.

These keys can dismantle everything that has allowed the unsurrendered souls of believers to sink down deep roots of fear and pain out of traumatic memories. This dismantling is accomplished by loosing the denial, the defenses, and the deceptions that have kept God's grace and mercy out of these deep, dark hiding places within us.

God will not override our defense systems. That would be a violation of our wills, regardless of whether it was done in the name of divine love or necessity of living. The wounded people of today have already been violated greatly, and God will not violate any who have confessed faith, hope, and trust in His only begotten Son. We must know how to take down our walls and strongholds, pulling up the final layers of self-protection, self-defense, and self-reliance that are guarding our areas of vulnerability. Only then can the One who is able to make us whole, Jesus Christ, move in and heal us.

Cooperating With Your Own Healing and Deliverance

No matter what books you've read, what seminars you've attended, or what groups you belong to— analyzing and working through <u>what your unsurrendered soul chooses to reveal to you</u> will not heal you. Only Jesus Christ can heal you. He stands at the door of our lives and knocks, speaking words of love, waiting patiently, seeking permission to gently enter the most private, hidden places of our pain without terrifying us. It is up to us to draw back the bolts and dismantle the self-defensive security systems of those places and let Him in!

Our wills' soulish defense systems have built strongholds which only served to exalt themselves between us and God! Personal, inner strongholds are the arguments, reasoning, logic, rationalization, justification, and denial we use to protect our wrong beliefs that help us deny what we <u>do not believe</u> we can change—what we <u>do not want</u> to change—what we <u>are afraid to try</u> to change about ourselves! These strongholds are our human reasoning and self-justification that say we are the way we are because of what has been done to us—we cannot be who God says we can be because of what has been done to us—we cannot do what God says we can do because of what has been done to us. All lies! These self-deceptions must be destroyed, smashed, and shattered!

Shattering Your Strongholds was the beginning, the breaking through of the unsurrendered soul's front line of defense. Now, in *Breaking the Power,* it is time to completely dismantle and deconstruct the unsurrendered soul's final line of defense—the layers upon layers of self-denial, self-reliance, self-protection, and self-defense over our unmet needs, unhealed hurts, and unresolved issues. Once these sources of all of our pain and fear are exposed, God can fill these leaking holes in our souls with His grace and mercy and love which will heal us. Only then can God move our souls into perfect alignment with our bodies and our spirits.

Only one human being ever walked the face of this earth in that perfect synergy of God's planned alignment of the human body, soul, and spirit. And He walked on water, healed the sick, raised the dead, and caused the eyes of the blind to see. He did this through a divine alignment of His body, soul, and spirit, thereby creating the perfect conduit to receive supernatural, miracle-working power. *Synergy* is defined (paraphrased from *Webster's Dictionary*) as the simultaneous action of individual agencies working perfectly together which results in a greater total effect than the combined sum of their individual effects. That's a mouthful, isn't it? In other words, if our bodies, souls, and spirits were each capable of one effect, when all three of them were working together in perfect "synergy," the sum total of their efforts would not be limited to three effects. It could be five, fifty, or maybe one hundred effects!

Jesus operated perfectly and powerfully in so many interactive realms, the three parts of His humanity (His body, soul, and spirit) and within the three parts of the Holy Trinity. He spoke things and did miracles that amazed and confounded the people of His day, and then He said that we are to be like Him in all His ways during our days here on earth. There is one Scripture I used to try not to think about too much, Romans 8:17. In part, this verse says, *"We must share His suffering if we are to share His glory"* (AMP). That verse always made me think, "Who wants to suffer being crucified like Jesus? Not me."

This word "suffering" (suffer, KJV) as used here means so much more than we've understood. Its original Greek meaning was <u>to experience evil, trouble, and persecution in a like manner with another</u> (*Thayer's Greek-English Lexicon).* I have known several people who were so terrified of having to suffer if they got close enough to Jesus to share part of His glory, that they deliberately kept a measure of distance between themselves and Him. What this verse is actually telling us is this: The evil, troubles, and persecutions that everyone in the world will go through anyway, can be experienced in the same manner of peace, faith, and grace that Jesus went through them with.

Jesus himself said God would finish this work in us that He had started. But God cannot finish us until our souls are in His desired alignment with our bodies and spirits. Such an alignment in a believer will manifest itself in a Christian who can walk and talk like Jesus did, raise people from the dead like Jesus did, and perform miracles even greater than Jesus Christ did. Never forget: Jesus is the One who said we were supposed to do exactly that! (See John 14:12.)

More Training-Wheel Prayers

This book is filled with "training-wheel prayers." There are more of them in *Breaking the Power* than there are in *Shattering Your Strongholds*. Training-wheel prayers are used to help you learn how to get your balance and your forward motion in a new way of praying—then you can kick them off and "go for it" on your own! Since new scriptural principles can sometimes seem so difficult to understand and use by those who most need them, the training-wheel prayers are designed to help anyone and everyone begin to immediately pray effectively against their souls' control over their lives. I believe God desires for this book to be a simple, fully understandable, user-friendly, hands-on victory manual with examples of personal applications of the deeper principles of the keys of the Kingdom.

I received what I considered to be high praise of the blood, sweat, and tears I invested in making these principles as understandable and available to everyone as I could in my first book. One native American woman of the Cherokee tribe gave a powerful word to me at one of my "24-Hour Invasions." She walked up to me, looked directly into my eyes, and said, "I know this book is of God because it's doable." Then she turned and walked away. I don't believe she said anything else to me the whole weekend. Yet I felt more blessed by her words, that my writings of the simplicity of God's Word were considered "doable," than I did over any other words of praise I've received since.

Many of the words in the training-wheel prayers are taken directly from the Scriptures, for I strongly believe in the power of praying the written words of the living Word, Jesus Christ. These prayers are deliberately written to be thought-provoking. Pray over the wording, the new ideas, and any passages that send you to the Scriptures to see if you can prove them as being valid. Think and meditate on the concepts, the phrases, and the words of these prayers. Above all, pray them from your heart; don't just read them with your mouth. Although, I have been amazed to find that even just reading them has brought beginnings steps of liberty into some lives!

Readjust the wording in any prayer to better fit your style of expressing yourself to the Father. Readjust the pronouns from "I" and "me" to others' names in any of the prayers in order to use them in intercession. Your soul will probably struggle with them at first; and when you pray them with and for others, their souls will probably struggle with them, too. The unsurrendered human soul does not like to be exposed as controlling and manipulating, especially when a person is convinced he or she has committed everything to Jesus Christ.

If you really have a conflict with most of the concepts in these prayers, at least bind your will to the will of God and your mind to the mind of Christ. Then loose the control out of your soul and all hindrances and devices of the enemy out of your life, both of which are used to confuse and unsettle you.

My prayer "lab rats" (as they were so affectionately identified in *Shattering Your Strongholds)* have been praying together with me, using the newer understandings of this book, over the past three years. We've confirmed something wonderful. Binding and loosing prayers just keep working and working! They truly are the keys to the Kingdom of God!

Liberty Savard

1

Don't Look Back For Your Destiny

Since I began using the keys of the Kingdom, I have moved into a new understanding of just how little I have to do with my destiny. As I was completing this book, I ran across a notation in my journal from June 29, 1994: *I have begun to ask myself the question of whether or not it is time to begin writing the second book. This morning, I saw myself as if I were viewing the world from deep inside a gun barrel. I think I am a bullet in there. All I can do is be a bullet, for it is God alone who can drop the hammer on the gun. I cannot pull the trigger from inside the barrel.*

God is in control of our destiny and nothing and no one in the world can alter His purposes for it. We can affect the amount of time we will have to actually walk in the fullness of this destiny while still on earth. But regardless of how much time we waste here by struggling with ourselves and our issues, we <u>will</u> step into the plans God has always had for us—even if it is only for a brief moment of time.

1

God has predestined certain "chapter headings" in our lives. We can choose to spend most of our lives trying to write, messing up, and then trying to rewrite our first chapter out of our own understanding and resources. Or we can choose to allow God to guide us so we can move gracefully and gloriously from chapter to chapter. The length of the journey, not the final destination, always keeps coming back to the choices we make. We think we are human beings having a spiritual experience on earth. We need to understand that we are spiritual beings for all time and eternity who happen to be having a little human experience on earth.

Sowing and Reaping

We all have the same exact choices of receiving or refusing what Jesus Christ has provided for us. Our pasts, our presents, and our futures as believers are all about the seeds sown by the choices we make. There are many Scriptures about sowing and reaping that most Christians understand with regard to seeds they sow. Galatians 6:7 (AMP) tells us, " . . . *Whatsoever a man sows, that and that only is what he will reap.*" But, if we did not sow the seeds of abuse and lack into our own lives in earlier years, then we do not have to reap from them today.

We've all had imperfect people in our pasts—people who (because of their own imperfect people) never knew how to meet our needs, heal our hurts, or resolve our confusion while our characters were being formed. We do not have to continue reaping today from their imperfect acts of yesterday. When we do not sow the seeds, we do not have to embrace the harvest fallout.

There is, however, a sowing-and-reaping cycle from our pasts that we must break. This is the cycle we

2

perpetuate by our verbal and mental replaying, reinforcing, and restating of the anger, confusion, fear, and unforgiveness still thriving in our souls! What happened to us decades ago lives on today only in memories in our minds. These memories (filled with emotions, fears, wrong attitudes, and skewed perceptions) provide the power supply our unsurrendered souls draw upon to control and manipulate our lives today.

Therapy, support, and love can help you learn to cope with old memories, but nothing can "neutralize" the power of those memories except the grace of God. You can cooperate with your own divine liberation by voluntarily destroying the strongholds and defense systems that have denied God any access to the inner depths of your soul's pain. He will not force His way into those areas. When access is offered to Him, however, He can and quickly will neutralize the stinging power of old memories by the greater power of His grace. This cooperation through faith is effected by loosing the wrong beliefs, attitudes, unforgiveness, soul-ties, layers of self-protection, and strongholds between you and God's plan for your freedom.

Different Beginnings

Each one of us was born into a completely different set of circumstances. All kinds of debits and credits were posted to our human ledgers before we ever landed in our doctors' hands. Some came into a family that did not know how to love. Some entered families where a single parent worked and no one was ever around to nurture them. Some landed in life on the "wrong" side of the tracks, some into poor families, some into performance-oriented families, some into totally

3

dysfunctional families. We all received certain family assets and liabilities before we ever took our first breaths.

When you're in the world without Jesus, these generational debits and credits can really give you a bad time. You can go through life with things hanging over your head, never understanding why you're always "losing out," why you're always having to make excuses for not measuring up. Non-believers may spend their entire lives trying to overcome negative beginnings, or they may just surrender to them and drop out of the "race" entirely.

When you became a Christian, you were born into a new family with a new spiritual parentage and bloodline. No longer do you have to live under any liabilities from your natural heritage. No longer do you have to try to figure out who you are or who you can be based upon your genes, your psychological makeup, or the environment in which you were raised. The only problem you, as a believer, may still have today is knowing how to let go of your self-perceived human limitations in order to begin living as a new creature in full relationship with God.

Many have a flawed concept of what their relationship with God is all about. Their view of God is framed by old mind-sets that were formed from their dealings with the authority figures of their pasts, rather than the truth of God's character today and forever. God's Word tells us that He sees us as His children, which should be viewed as a wonderful opportunity. But this blessed truth can produce a very "frightened child/ imperfect parent" struggle with God if we view Him through our souls' cloudy filters of the imperfect human relationships we may have known. Such cloudy filters can be clogged with unreasonable fear, which produces guilt, which produces more fear, and so on. What we have experienced in our pasts can become carved in stone as mind-sets of fear and suspicion towards any form of authority.

Did you ever stop to think that everything you have ever learned about God has had to filter down through wrong beliefs, ideas, and attitudes already existing in your mind before you ever knew Him? Unless you know how to clean out the filters of your soul (accomplished by loosing prayers), those wrong beliefs and attitudes can remain in conflict with every new truth presented to you. You can't get <u>anything</u> to pass through fear/deception/pain-clogged filters and come out pure. Not even God's truth.

This fact is not always understood by Christians. Many Christians, including those in leadership, assume that scripturally-correct teaching will automatically and immediately clear up any wrong ideas someone might have about God. And it will—eventually—after God has had to take some of us around Mount Sinai about 3,000 times. Even then, some of us still have to take extra laps!

When you finally stop seeing yourself in terms of your past—unhappy beginnings, shattered marriages, lost jobs, poverty, and so forth—you can begin to see the potential of your future as a child of God. You begin to recognize that you are destined to be strong and whole, with signs and wonders following you everywhere you go. If you are not seeing that yet, then you have been opposing yourself and opposing God because of strongholds in your old nature.

Letting Go of My Past

I came into Christianity some twenty-five years ago, understanding only the rules and regulations. There were plenty of "thou shalt do's" and "thou shalt do not's" in my church, plus I think they made up a few new ones for their own protection when I got saved there. I assure the people I speak to across the United States that they should be glad I didn't get saved in their churches, for I did not come gently into the Body of Christ. I came in as a mad, hostile, hurting, militant feminist who was ready to straighten things out. I immediately saw the main problem in the church I landed in—it was all of those "chauvinists" up on the platform. And I decided I was anointed to show them the error of their ways!

If that wasn't enough to get me into hot water, I believed from the beginning of my Christian experience that I was called to be in the ministry. When I told my mainline, traditional church leaders that, they nearly had heart attacks! I have always suspected that one pastor in particular called secret prayer meetings where many prayed, "No, God, no! She'll fry the lambs and singe the sheep! Please, God, no!"

I was not a very happy camper in those days. I felt the world didn't understand me, my family had no idea what I wanted, and my church didn't want me in the ministry. I went through some pretty serious, spiritual mid-life crises during the first ten years I was saved. I also personally helped solidify several pastors' callings by establishing them in their ministries in those early days. It was a case of get hold of God or get out of the ministry when they had to deal with me. One day a pastor said to me, "Liberty, you have a sandpaper ministry!" I was just so excited that he thought I had a ministry, I didn't even realize what he'd just said.

Don't "write off" the "troublemakers" in your church, at least not until they've remained troublemakers for decades. Pray for them and try to love them as much as you can, for they're trying to find out the hard way what works and what doesn't. After I was saved, I loved Jesus, I wanted to be used of God, but I was still causing problems in my church for nearly thirteen years! The church leaders put me in the choir, in the nursery, and in the parking lot, trying to keep me where someone knew what I was doing at all times. Ultimately they had to take the big leap, and they put me in the church office where they could all watch me at once.

Many probably wanted to write me off in those early years, but there were a special, precious few who didn't give up on me. I don't know if they saw something in me, if they thought I was a good missions project, or if they just felt sorry for me. But they didn't give up on me. That's God's grace in action!

Enough of This Carnal Stuff!

In 1985, after some thirteen-plus years of being frustrated, I was suddenly maxed out with the spiritual walk I was walking—a walk of powerless clichés and aching emptiness. I began to spend hours on my knees beside my bed crying out, "God, I don't care what you have to do: melt me, break me, smash me, crush me, mold me however you want. I can't go on the way I am any longer." I had a form of godliness, but no power—no joy, no peace, and no hope that my life would ever change and get better. What I began to desperately cry out that day in 1985 began to change my life. I had no clue that I was "loosing" bondage and walls out of my soul (see Greek definitions of loose in opening "Bridge").

However small a beginning it was, I had given God a little crack of access into my self-constructed defense system. God started talking to me right away about binding and loosing in a brand new way. From that point on, the crack just kept slowly getting bigger and bigger. New revelation and right understanding about misconceptions I had about God and my Christian walk began to trickle into my spirit. I struggled alone with this slowly growing understanding for two more years, being the only "one" who seemed to see the meaning of what I felt God was saying.

Being very opinionated, strong-willed, and aggressive when I first landed in my church in 1972 (can you believe I'm still a part of that same church in 1997?), I had suffered many self-inflicted wounds from the "shooting-oneself-in-the-foot" syndrome. In 1985, when the initial understanding of the true power in binding and loosing began unfolding to me, I had learned not to rock boats, question established doctrine, or challenge the teachings of authorities over me. I tried to ignore the new ideas I kept hearing, but the nudgings of God continued day after day.

It was the late fall of 1987 before I officially went "public" with this new understanding. I prayed and asked God for an opportunity to take the message to people who didn't know me (I wasn't afraid of strangers). In three days, I received four out-of-town speaking engagements. I accepted them, and went and preached the new ways to use binding and loosing on the unsurrendered soul. At the first meeting, nearly everyone choked up on the concept. It got a little better at each following meeting.

Some were opposed outright, some were doubtful, some were just confused. As might be expected, many negative remarks and comments were made. But one delightfully encouraging remark did come forth the first night. Two young women ran up to me after the teaching and simultaneously cried out, "We want to do it! Do we bind or loose it?" They had no idea how to apply the teaching they had just heard, but a very important facet of spiritual success was already in place in their spirits. If God's Word said it, they believed it, they wanted to get in on it, they wanted to do it! They recognized the teaching message was from the Word, and they mixed their faith with what they heard.

Many people have asked me, "Why haven't we heard this before?"

My only answer is, "I don't know, *but you're hearing it now*! What are you going to do about it from this point on?"

Matthew 16:19 tells us that Jesus said, *"I will give unto thee the keys of the kingdom of heaven and whatsoever thou shalt bind on earth shall be bound in heaven and whatsoever thou shalt loose on earth shall be loosed in heaven"* (KJV). The church world got so enamored with the word *bind* here, they ignored the word right in front of it—whatsoever. They didn't stop to realize the scope of this principle, for there is no limitation to this word *whatsoever.* It covers anything and everything.

Truth and Faith Is Powerful!

There are many today who are searching for fresh understanding of how to finally be free of their old natures and their souls' hidden agendas. These are the ones who desire to become a new breed of prayer warriors, free of soulish hindrances and personal strongholds. These new prayer warriors will go far beyond anything I have yet to imagine as coming out of this message's goal of getting

9

people ready to receive the prophetic word from the end-time prophets now rising up. Their prophetic message will be the one that rocks the Church and shocks the world in these final days.

Paul said in Hebrew 4:2 (AMP), *"For indeed we have had the glad tidings of God proclaimed to us just as truly as they (the Israelites of old did when the good news of deliverance from bondage came to them); but the message they heard did not benefit them, because it was not mixed with faith (that is, with the leaning of the entire personality on God in absolute trust and confidence in His power, wisdom and goodness) by those who heard it . . . ."*

You must mix your faith with this word and say to your soul, "This is so good, I'm going to do it!" If you don't, the words you read here will not benefit you for long. The anointing, the power, and the understanding will dissipate because you did not act on the principles and make them yours. You can begin to use these principles right now, make them your truth, and be more than ready the next time crisis hits. By virtue of use, you can turn these words into your personal truth, and they will become your keys to handle anything the devil, the world, your family, or others throw at you.

So Where Do You Begin?

One of the first things God taught me was to bind my will to His will. When I questioned Him as to whether I could really bind my unruly, rascally, rebellious, "free" will to His will, I received the impression of these words: *"Like it had magnets!"* Binding my will to God's will produced an incredible steadiness in my spiritual walk.

Suddenly, I had a sense of balance, a stability in my steps that I had never had.

Then He said to bind my mind to the mind of Christ. "Oh, God, I've tried so hard to get His mind in me, but my mind is so full of stuff that I can't seem to get out." But He had said to do it and I did, and the three "VCRs" in my mind went into freeze frame for just a minute. They started back up again, but I saw a glimmer of hope. There was more to come that would finish that off.

Then He told me to bind myself to an awareness of the blood of Jesus Christ because I often forgot what the power of His blood had done for me. I did this and for a period of time, I would occasionally "see" a red sheet come over my eyes. I know this was a new awareness of the blood, and I would always burst into tears. I really startled some people in a couple of grocery stores when that happened!

Then He had me bind my feet to the paths He had always ordained for me to walk. I asked, "Like they had magnets?"

He said, *"Like they had magnets."* He told me to bind my hands to the work He had always meant for me to do in order to prosper His will in the Kingdom, and I did. He said to bind myself to the work of the Cross, because that was where the power, the authority, the love, the forgiveness, the mercy, and the grace would flow into my life. I did, and it was good!

I realized that, regardless of how much I had previously been praying as I thought I should, I had been off-track for years. God was trying to show me how to get every one of my prayers answered every time. Wow, what a concept! As simple as it sounds, I believe this is one of the most profound things I have ever recognized about prayer. James 4:3 (KJV) says, *"Ye ask* [pray], *and receive not, because ye ask amiss . . . . "* The Greek word for *amiss* means "wrongly." We can get all of our prayers answered every time by praying right prayers.

Warning Bells and Whistles

Does binding your will to God's will mean you will never step out of it again? No. Binding your will to God's will means that you will no longer be able to rationalize, justify, and deny making a wrong choice without having a big fanfare and fuss right in your face! I bind my will to God's will every day, often many times, and when I try to justify pursuing my own will, the bells and whistles go off. A warning barricade comes down in front of me like a railroad crossing barrier. Then I must deliberately choose whether or not to climb over or crawl under that barricade and sprint out onto the tracks, ignoring any oncoming freight train. I must choose to disobey God with my eyes wide open and my mind fully aware of impending consequences. It is amazing how clearly I can usually see the better choice in His will.

If we truly want God's will, we must be willing to accept the results of it—whether we understand those results or not. When God tries to bring something powerful but different into our lives in order to use us in new ways, we're often startled and fearful, crying out, "Why is this happening?" We particularly fuss when He tries to use us in some way that doesn't fit into what we've learned are the expectable, acceptable, and humanly permissible perimeters for His dealings with us.

Mary, Jesus' mother, didn't "understand" what she was about to face, but surely she must have been concerned about being an unwed, pregnant woman in a culture that reacted so vehemently to illegitimacy. Yet Mary listened to the words of the angel Gabriel with her spirit and made the choice to accept the will of God regardless of what would happen to her. I believe God poured untold grace into her in order to strengthen and empower her, and to neutralize the anxiety and fear her soul must have tried to unleash.

Therein lay the key to Mary's victory. She made the choice to go forth with God regardless of human, natural consequences, and she received divine empowerment of great grace and strength to be used in a way that no human being had ever yet been used.

Her spirit heard exactly what the angel was saying and accepted it without question and without any negotiating for more details. You see, it is not our spirits that cry out for details and security deposits when God stretches us. It is our souls—our minds, wills, and emotions—that drive us to try to "own" and thereby imprint some form of control over what God is doing with our lives.

Supernatural and Practical

Truth won't do you any good if you're afraid to appropriate it, handle it, chew on it, and use it. So many people say, "Well, I know it must be true. I understand that in my head, and I'm trying to get it down into my heart." That's the wrong direction! Your mind doesn't understand, nor is it willing to learn, anything from God's Spirit. The understanding of God's truth and absolute trustworthiness can only be imparted into your inner man, into your spirit, by the Holy Spirit of God. Your spirit then wants to impart it up to the natural awareness of your mind.

This is often thwarted by the mind being full of soulish thoughts and beliefs. Loosing wrong thoughts and beliefs, reading the Word, praising the Lord, and prayer prepare you to receive from Him. He'll put the understanding into your spirit and it will flash all through you. I have one particularly mundane little testimonial about that. The more old, unnecessary "stuff" that I loose out of my own soul, the more room I have to receive God's practical as well as miraculous revelation .

Recently both toilets in my house began to run. As my landlord lives over 100 miles away, I kept thinking I would get someone local to fix them. But I never seemed to remember to do it, and the toilets just kept running. Then one morning, after a week of much loosing and stripping of trivia from my mind, I awoke with a sudden, full knowledge of exactly what was wrong, why it was wrong, what to do about it, and where to purchase the parts needed to do just that. I had been using some high-strength bleach tablets for the water tanks in both of the toilets, and these tablets had eventually hardened and warped those little "stopper things" in the tanks. I drove to the local hardware store, picked out new "stopper things" and installed them myself. I was quite impressed with God's information, for even I was able to implement it.

When God gives you information that requires action, you must act on it or your toilets will just keep running! You can have all the knowledge and faith in the world, but if you sit in a corner with it and never act on it—your faith is dead and useless. (Read James 2:17.) Taking an action of faith does not always mean becoming a missionary or going to Bible school or preaching on a street corner. Sometimes taking an action is simply taking a stand of faith when you have done everything else you know to do. Taking action can be a verbal loosing of negative, fearful, discouraging thoughts that leap into your mind

14

when the going gets rough. Taking action on your faith can be a strong, purposeful rejection of anything that does not line up with God's Word. Taking action can be a verbal binding of yourself to God's will and purposes, to His truth, and to the mind of Christ—refusing to be moved into any decision that does not line up with His Word.

Once you have steadied yourself through these very real acts of faith and brought your own soul into some form of submission, God can give you the next step—answers and deliverance. But as long as you allow your unsurrendered soul to muddy the waters and fill your mind with strongholds, it may be a long time before you receive the "next step." Faith does indeed come by hearing the Word of truth, but faith grows and progresses by experiencing the Word of truth. Strongholds are designed to protect what you already believe and to reject everything else. You won't act on or learn to experience anything you have chosen to reject.

One Final Checkpoint!

How do you know if I am telling the truth? Not by listening to your soul, for sure! I have never forgotten a training experience I had some thirty years ago when I became a bank teller. I was warned that if I took in any counterfeit bills, I would have to make them good. That really scared me, and I asked my trainer to show me some counterfeit bills so I could learn to recognize them. The trainer just gave me stacks and stacks of money to count and wrap, hour after hour, day after day. I had to look at so much money that I was dreaming in green! Several days later, I was moved onto the open teller line.

15

I worriedly reminded my trainer, "But you never showed me what a counterfeit bill looks like!"

The trainer told me not to worry, adding, "Your best defense against accepting a counterfeit is to be so familiar with the real thing that a counterfeit automatically sets off a warning when you see it." And that is exactly what happened to me at a future date. The trainer had so immersed me in the "real" thing, when a counterfeit bill came through, I instantly knew it was not right.

That is an excellent truth for Christians as well. Everyone is trying to learn what the latest cults and New Age doctrines are, and there is nothing wrong with that. But believers can't possibly know every false religion, every cult's deceptions, every New Age nuance today. You can only become so familiar with the real thing—God's Word—that anything counterfeit will jump out at you. If you're immersed in the Word of God, when something phony comes along, you might not know what's wrong with it—but you'll definitely smell something fishy!

2

Body, Soul, Spirit, and Strongholds

God seems to like threes. He functions in a threefold unity himself—as the divine Father, Son, and Holy Ghost. And He designed you and me to function as a three-part being consisting of a body, a soul, and a spirit. Your body relates to the earth and its environment through your natural senses of hearing, sight, smell, taste, and touch. It likes to feel good and be comfortable—with plenty of great food, sleep and relaxation, sensory stimulation, comfort, pleasure, touchy/feely good stuff, etc. Whenever these requirements are being basically met, the body will go along with whoever or whatever appears to be in charge.

Your spirit is that part of you that relates to God's Spirit. It wants to be in relationship with its Creator. When you asked Jesus Christ to save you, forgive you, and wash you in His blood, your spirit was put back into relationship with the Spirit of God. It became and remains blessed, forgiven, and ecstatic about this position. When it finally gets the rest of you to listen to the revelations it is receiving from God and to surrender to His plans and purposes for your destiny, your body and soul will live every day blessed, forgiven, and ecstatic, too!

Your soul—a three-part existence of mind, will, and emotions—is meant to be in perfect alignment with God's will and purposes for your whole being. But the soul is not really open to such an idea, for it is this part of you that strongly resists following or surrendering. It wants to be the final word on all "system" decisions, overruling any input from your body, your spirit, God, or anyone else! It's no wonder a believer can feel so undone at times.

In the beginning, God's Spirit communicated through man's spirit to his soul which jointly acted out, or manifested, God's divine will through the clay vessel of man's body. After the Fall in the Garden of Eden resulting from Adam and Eve partaking of the fruit of the tree of the knowledge of good and evil (in direct disobedience to God's command), man's spirit was cut off from the communion it had known with God's Spirit. His spirit lost its ability to function with unction from above. The human soul, either by desire or by default (I'm not sure which), took over running things based upon its new intellectual and emotional understanding of good and evil. Bad choice!

I believe the human spirits of all men and women ever since have felt lost, helpless, and needy, just like spiritual orphans, wanting only to be reunited with their Creator's Spirit.

From Adam and Eve on through every ensuing generation, each part of mankind's triune being was now skewed and misaligned from its original purpose. Our souls are particularly misaligned, needing a definite adjustment from God's "holy chiropractor," the Holy Ghost. There's just one catch: God will not force that adjustment upon our souls, and our unsurrendered souls are generally quite adamant about not wanting their chosen courses of action to be adjusted. Mine doesn't, yours doesn't.

I cannot help but think of a very humorous (yet potentially disastrous) true story I heard about an actual radio transmission of a confrontation between American and Canadian authorities off the coast of Canada a few years ago. The names of the authorities and actual ship have been changed to protect the feelings of those involved.

US ship: Please divert your course 0.5 degrees to the South to avoid collision.

Canadian reply: Recommend you divert YOUR course 15 degrees to the South to avoid a collision.

US ship: This is the captain of the US Navy ship. I say again, divert YOUR course.

Canadian reply: No, I say again, divert YOUR course!

US ship: THIS IS THE AIRCRAFT CARRIER USS "* * *." WE ARE A LARGE WARSHIP OF THE US NAVY. DIVERT YOUR COURSE NOW!

Canadian reply: This is a lighthouse. Your call.

This is a perfect example of some of our souls' decisions to refuse any change of course when they believe they are right. Your soul wants to defend its free will on every side, building strongholds around its wrong beliefs, even though you may actually be heading straight to a crackup on rocky shores. As long as those strongholds are left intact, you're in a world of trouble. Strongholds lock lies and deceptions into your soul, along with your needs, hurts, and confusion.

God will not cross the walls of your self-constructed inner strongholds, so they keep His grace and healing out. But Satan and his spirits readily gain access to hammer on your soul through these same strongholds because you have built them in disobedience to God's will. Satan always shows up to take advantage of any act of disobedience to God that is not repented for, turned away from (dismantled in the case of strongholds), forgiven and washed in the blood of Jesus Christ. And evil spirits start working to compound the neediness, pain, and confusion of your wounded, unsurrendered soul that rages and ranges just beyond the control of the Holy Spirit. For this we can ask our "free will" to take a bow.

The Real Rebel

When I accepted Jesus Christ as my Savior, my spirit got saved. Just my spirit. It was delighted, delirious, and thrilled to be reunited with its Creator. It said, "I'm forgiven, hallelujah, glory to God, I'm a new creature—ahhhhhhhhhh! I am just going to lovvvvvvve everybody, I'm going to forgive everythinnnnnng anybody ever did to me. I'm going to give up every offense and bless everyone."

My unsurrendered soul said, "Say what? I've been keeping records of every mean thing that has been done to you, every wrong thing that has been said about you, and every single thing that has been taken from you. I have files on every offense! I have records, I have names, I have addresses. I have phone numbers! And I'm keeping every single one of them until I get even. Throw away my whole record-keeping system of everyone's injustice to you because you've had some religious experience with Jesus? I think not!

"I'm the one who has kept everything stored and alive for you, I'm the one who has carried the pain. Do you realize what I've been through to do this? And now you want me to just toss it all away? Not until I get even!"

Man's unsurrendered soul wants to get even, and there is a multibillion-dollar legal industry today that has fed off that desire. A lot of money can be made off the soul's unfulfilled desires. Very little money can be made off the regenerated spirit. No wonder the world doesn't cater to God's plans. Although your spirit gloriously basked in the forgiveness and the cleansing of your new birth, your soul wasn't about to let go of its records of betrayal, unforgiveness, painful memories, anger, and resentment. Your spiritual salvation caused it to back up and dig in for the fight of its life. Philippians 2:12 (AMP) speaks of the ongoing process of the soul's salvation: *". . . Work out—cultivate, carry out to the goal and fully complete—your own salvation with reverence and awe and trembling [self-distrust, that is, with serious caution, tenderness of conscience, watchfulness against temptation; timidly shrinking from whatever might offend God and discredit the name of Christ]."*

2 Corinthians 10:5 (KJV) tells us that we should be: *"Casting down imaginations, and every high thing that exalteth itself against the knowledge of God . . . ."* *Thayer's Greek/English Lexicon* says this means to throw down, demolish, and destroy, <u>with violence and force</u>, the barriers, ramparts, and bulwarks between you and your knowledge of God. Our soul thinks its job

description is to throw up arguments, reasonings, and logic—strongholds—to keep us from having a true knowledge of God. Our spirit-man's job description is to pull every high thing down the soul throws up—with the violence and force inherent in God's spiritual principles when we combine those principles with faith and action.

Why Do We Build Strongholds?

Why do people build strongholds in the first place? Generally, it is because the strongholds enabled them to survive circumstances in their pasts that were out of their control. Strongholds allowed them to alter their perception of a reality that they simply did not know how to process. For example, when a child is badly abused by a parent, the child's entire safety structure is threatened if he or she believes the abusing parent truly meant harm. Few children have the emotional and mental capabilities to process that kind of betrayal. So, the child may alter reality into something he or she can deal with.

Quite often, that turns into the concept that the abuse was their own fault—if they had only been better, the parent wouldn't have been forced to hurt them. Most abused children know how to process that scenario. This is the beginning of a twisted logic and reasoning (self-constructed stronghold) in abused children that if they could just learn to be perfect, they could exert a form of control over out-of-control people around them. That is, of course, incorrect. But it seems to work enough that children "logically" begin to reason that perfectionism is their best shot at avoiding further abuse.

And the stronghold is put in place.

The child becomes an adult, never realizing it is a lie that by behaving perfectly he or she can change or control the behavior of other people around them. This type of reasoning exists in battered wives, spouses of alcoholics, and other codependent relationships: "If I hadn't done this, or if I hadn't said that, he (or she) wouldn't have done such and such." Until that stronghold is dismantled and released, it will always impair the person's life.

Once we have locked a certain set of logic, rationalizations, and justifications in place, we become static and we stop growing. The rigidity of these stronghold defenses keeps us from becoming who God says we can be: victorious Christians, peacemakers, and overcomers who are whole, courageous, filled with power, and able to impart healing and grace to others. These are roles we should have automatically moved into as soon as we accepted Christ. Our spirits were ready to, but our souls weren't—they were filled with too much worldly conditioning, too many old memories, too many open wounds, and too many fears.

Preventive Soul Maintenance

How do you avoid setting up new strongholds in yourself? Anger, fear, and pain are all cause for great alarm in the unsurrendered soul, initiating stronghold-building on all fronts. Let's consider anger as one cause. Be very aware whenever anyone offends, insults, lies to, or tricks you. Because of wrong beliefs, attitudes, and patterns of thinking that you have learned, you can react to the offense with indignation and anger. When you choose to justify and rationalize your anger over an offense (no matter how big in your eyes) as a right thing to have and hold onto, it becomes rebellion, disobedience, and sin as soon as the sun goes down. (See Eph. 4:26.) God has said that your anger is to be dealt with before the sun goes down, which gives you a maximum time period of twenty-three hours, fifty-nine minutes and fifty-nine seconds to let it go.

Don't ever try to justify self-righteous anger by calling it a holy anger. Holy anger is much rarer than you think. Jesus did exhibit holy anger when He overturned the money changers' tables in His Father's temple. His soul was fully surrendered to God. Moses did not exhibit holy anger when he struck the rock in the desert. Great man of God that Moses was, he was still capable of acting out of soulish frustration when he was under great pressure.

Qualify and clarify the following fact for yourself in advance of having to deal with angry feelings that will come. Nearly all of the time, your anger will be self-righteous. Getting this settled up front will help you to recognize when your feelings are slipping out of a godly way of thinking. Don't try to analyze or justify being angry, just begin to loose the angry feelings in order to pull your emotions and thoughts back into alignment with God's will for you. Bind your mind to the mind of Christ and loose all wrong thoughts about personal rights and what is or is not "fair." Don't listen to your soul screaming, "Foul!"

Self-righteous anger is an emotional symptom of wrong beliefs and wrong thinking deeply rooted within unhealed pain in your soul. Anger is never godly if you feel personally offended, slighted, or wronged in any way.

This can be a slippery area to traverse, for your soul is a master at "religious rationalization" of your feelings. Your soul can come up with a very convincing argument that you are only angry because someone is speaking or acting against Christians or God himself. This is why binding yourself to God's truth in any given situation, while loosing wrong beliefs and their strongholds, is important in order to bring truth into focus.

Your soul's internal chant is, "No more pain—no more pain—no more pain." As it attempts to enforce this dogma, it begins to put down layers of self-defense, self-protection, and self-denial over the areas of your greatest vulnerability. This is like burying radioactive material under your home! It might appear to be out of sight, but the dangerous, toxic, radioactive emissions keep coming up into your everyday existence.

What God Won't Do for You

Many people have told me, "I don't believe I have to pray binding and loosing prayers about my strongholds. I just ask God to take them down for me." This won't work, regardless of what your soul has told you. You build self-protective strongholds out of a decision of your own will. No matter how hard you pray, God <u>will not override and undo</u> a rebellious act of your will! But He <u>will pressure you to address and reverse</u> your own willfulness that erects the strongholds in the first place.

Some people, especially those who have a lot of strongholds in their lives, resist praying the binding and loosing training-wheel prayers. They say they don't want to pray "vain, repetitious" written prayers. God has no problems with repetitious prayers and His Holy Spirit

moved upon nearly every man who recorded the Holy
Scriptures to write down many prayers. Second Timothy
3:16 (don't you just love the 3:16's of the Bible?) tells
us this: *"All scripture is given by inspiration of God,
and is profitable for doctrine, for reproof, for correction,
for instruction in righteousness"* (KJV). This includes
the written prayers.

God does have a problem with *vain* prayers,
however, whether they are one-time, intermittent,
repetitious, written, or otherwise! The word "vain" (and
its root meaning) that Jesus used in Matthew 6:7 to
describe prayers we should not pray is defined as prayers
that are "pure folly, having no purpose, attempting to
handle or to squeeze, and to try to manipulate." There is
nothing vain or manipulative in the use of the binding
and loosing prayer principles. The only thing these
prayers will squeeze is your old carnal nature, hallelujah!

I once heard a young African evangelist say his
ministry message was PUSH, an acronym for PRAY
UNTIL SOMETHING HAPPENS. He said, "You
Americans, you pray until nothing happens and then you
go try something else. In Africa, we don't have all those
options, and we have to pray until something happens."
A good word, indeed! Give the binding and loosing
training-wheel prayers a good honest run in your life.
Don't just pray and give up twenty-four hours later. Pray
until something happens!

I really struggled to believe that God would never
say to me, "I don't want to hear another word about that,
so don't bug me anymore." God tells us to go ahead and
bug Him—just as long as our prayers are not vain, having
hidden agendas or manipulative motives. Pray without
ceasing, persevere in prayer, continue in prayer, press

26

through in prayer, pray written prayers from the Bible and elsewhere if you can learn from them. Pray all of your normal, regular prayers—prayers you feel comfortable with and prayers that stretch you. But as you pray, add in some form or version of the binding and loosing training-wheel prayers for a few weeks and just see what happens. Always remember that Matthew 16:19 says, *"Whatsoever you bind/loose on earth will be bound/ loosed in heaven."*

Have I finally surrendered my soul into a full submission to God's will and ways, or do I still struggle with some strongholds? I must, because the last time I tried to walk on water, I almost drowned! Actually, I'm not aware of any scary, overwhelming strongholds anymore. But I am still dealing with smaller ones—sort of like the little foxes that spoil the grapes if you don't get them out of your land. I've been delighted to realize that rooting out of most of the big foxes, and some little hidden foxes as well, has touched every area of my being. I have a greater measure of peace in my mind, flexibility in my will, and balance in my emotions. I have a higher level of spiritual discernment, and I have more physical stamina. Rarely do I seem to catch any of the viruses that infect people's bodies. Some of this multifaceted blessing is due to the fact that I'm turning less and less to external sources for comfort and energy (i.e., "The Big C's"—chocolate, cookies, and coffee!).

Got Any Struggles?

How do you know if you have a surrendered or an unsurrendered soul? If you struggle with any of the commandments, precepts, or principles of God's Word;

if you struggle with fear and doubt; if you struggle with any authority over you; if you struggle with any of your family members; if you struggle with any of your neighbors; if you struggle with waiting for anything; if you struggle with others moving ahead in God's ministry faster than you; if you struggle with being single; if you struggle with being married; if you struggle with anything—then you do have not have a surrendered soul. Get the picture?

To help us recognize when we're operating out of unsurrendered souls, God often brings us into serious situations where we can't mentally think our way out, emotionally manipulate our way out, or bull our way out through sheer determination of will. This is where we can end up crying and wailing that He's forsaken us and the devil is going to get us. But God is actually very close at those times, waiting for us to recognize the ultimate futility of our own attempts to be in the driver's seat and then turn to Him in full surrender.

The Vehicles Are Driving Themselves

Man, left to his own devices, will usually seek to elevate the importance of his mind, will, and emotions in the process of finding satisfaction and happiness. He may spend all he has to try to learn how to become the intellectual "master" of his own fate. One problem with this man-made theory of self-attainment is that life is sometimes full of emotionally unpredictable and intellectually uncontrollable crises that hit like tornadoes from above or earthquakes from below—with complete disregard for the strongest of human wills.

Our peace, satisfaction, and joy do not come from

within any part of us, they come from Jesus Christ dwelling in us. His peace and joy is the only kind of peace and joy that circumstances cannot touch. Unshakable, unchanging peace and joy are found in knowing Him better, not in knowing ourselves better. Actually, deep introspection, focused on inner fact-finding trips to "know oneself," can be quite dangerous. Your soul will accommodate you with whatever information or memories you want to help justify a wrong attitude, desire, or belief you have. Some false "memories" seem so real, only the Word and the Spirit can reveal the deception of them. (See Heb. 4:12.)

The soul in itself profits us nothing except as a vehicle of expression for our regenerated spirits. The human soul wants to drive, but it is simply the vehicle. It may be a Pinto or it may be a Rolls Royce, but it is still just a vehicle designed to <u>transport something more important than itself</u>. Our souls have attempted to usurp the roles of the vehicle owner, the driver, the mechanic, and the body shop. Our souls have attempted to mentally, emotionally, and willfully finesse or ram (whatever seems appropriate to them) their way through all the traffic jams of our lives. This brings confusion, stress, and anxiety to our entire makeup, including our body.

A whole lot of personal stress is relieved when we kick our souls out of the driver's seat and leave the driving to God. He is so good at it, it is ridiculous to fight Him for the wheel! To allow our souls any control over our lives only brings us frustration and misery. The following training-wheel prayer is designed to help you dismantle your soul's power and ability to manipulate your life.

29

Training-Wheel Prayer
for Breaking Soul Power

Bless the Lord, O my soul, with all that is within you. Bless His holy name! Soul, I bind you to your destiny as a fully integrated, divinely created part of God's purposes for my life. I loose the wrong beliefs, attitudes, patterns of thinking, control factors, self-centeredness, and layers you have protected and created to try to control my life.

I loose denial, deception, and discouragement from you. I loose the power of the word curses you have taken into your inner chambers and made your truth. I loose the power of the wrong agreements you've entered into and the soul-ties you have joined together with. I loose the effects of the generational-bondage thinking you have accepted as fact, whether received from the ungodly transference of evil spirits, from close association with unsurrendered human souls, or from ancestral ungodliness. Jesus Christ has made me free from all generational curses, and I am now enacting and speaking that truth into being in my own life. I bind myself to the full liberty that Christ has extended to me through the brand-new covenant relationship, new family heritage, and new bloodline that is now mine.

You, soul, were created by God to translate the revelations and manifest the workings of the Holy Spirit to the world—not to run my life. You have not yet begun to imagine the things that God has in store for you to accomplish when you come completely into alignment with His will and purposes for your existence. But you, my soul, are becoming a surrendered vehicle of divine expression. Through thoughts and words of life expressed out of my renewed mind, through supernatural peace and joy out of my renewed emotions, through a righteous and godly courage and boldness out of my renewed will, you—my soul—are going to bring forth understanding to many who do not know and have never understood God. Soul, I bind each part of you to God's will and purposes!

Mind, once you turned in circles like a rat caught in a maze, constantly going over and over negatives and fears about the decisions you did not have answers for, yet felt trapped into making. Remember the nightmares that terrorized you, coming from your confusion and hopelessness, nightmares that would not allow a peaceful night's sleep. Remember the unresolved issues you could not resolve and kept trying to bury, only they crawled up out of those graves again and again.

Mind, I bind you to the truth of the clarity of thought that God has touched you with now, to a realization of the divine interventions occurring all the time in the problems you could never solve, to the peace now possible in your sleep. Mind, I bind you to a grateful awareness of the wisdom and revelation that God is beginning to pour through you. You will be brought into a faithful and true alignment with God so that I will become one of those in the end times who are filled with understanding and able to teach others, as spoken of by the prophet Daniel. You will be used to show forth God's wisdom and revelation for understanding in these last days. You will be filled with divine understanding by the Holy Spirit to enable me to teach many who will not understand what has begun to happen, even though they search diligently

31

throughout God's Word. Bless the Lord, O my soul, and forget not His benefits.

Emotions, forget not how you once reeled between laughter and tears, boldness and fear, hope and despair, affection and anger. You frightened people away from me by either bordering on tears of neediness or outbursts of rage, and then you fed fuel to my feelings of rejection and loneliness within. But now, emotions, you are learning to receive divine peace, to express joy and hope, to respond to the Holy Spirit's lifting power when old, negative feelings try to ascend. I bind you, emotions, to the divine role you are to play in my life: Your unique ability to project God's peace and joy and hope to those who do not understand the promises of His Spirit. Bless the Lord, O my soul, and forget not His benefits.

Will, forget not the causes and the battles you used to engage in, always rigidly implacable and unrelenting in your stands. Unrepentant, unbending, unyielding, always unwilling to work with another's ideas, you alienated many. Will, you caused much grief with your stubbornness, resistance, and rebellion to God's ways. But now, my will, you are bound to the will of the Father. You are learning how to be strong, yet flexible; to be right, yet entreatable; to be bold, yet gentle; to be courageous, yet concerned for others. Only the Holy Spirit can perfectly balance each side of these strengths in me. I bind you, will, to the total and complete purposes and plans of the Lord. I bind you to the will of my heavenly Father.

Will, you shall show forth His courage, His boldness, and His fearlessness as you give me the backbone and assurance to stand in the face of danger and enemy attack, always knowing that He is Almighty God who loves me.

You shall come into alignment with His divine order for my destiny. Bless the Lord, O my soul, and forget not all His benefits.

I loose every wrong agreement from my soul. I cut asunder all soulish ties that my soul has sought, accepted, and expected to derive power from. I loose the wrong desires and motives that my soul has carefully protected and used to bring others into agreement with its deceptions. Soul, you will no longer derive power and ungodly satisfaction from drawing upon a soulish tie with another human being or with any evil spirit.

Soul, you will come into alignment with God's power and will. You will surrender the layers you've laid down over the deepest, darkest chambers within yourself. I loose your layers of self-control, self-denial, self-protectiveness, self-defense, and self-centeredness that you have piled over my most vulnerable areas that are so needful of God's grace. I loose the deceptions and the lies you are clinging to, the soulish guilt you have allowed to bring torment to me over things that were not my fault. I loose the deceptions you have hammered me with and have used to cause me to cave in to your control.

Lord, I strip away every layer and stronghold my soul has erected to keep you from getting into the darkness within its inner chambers. I ask you to pour your grace and mercy into these areas of need, hurt, and unresolved issues. I know that only you can fix them. I bind the inner parts of my soul to your truth, Father, so that your truth will always be the plumb line for the truing up of my mind, my emotions, and my will. I want your truth to be the straight edge of my life, the guiding light of my life, and the backbone of my soul.

Bless the Lord, O my soul, with all that is within you. Forget not His benefits. Remember what He has done for you! In Jesus' name, Amen.

Who's Taking Authority Here?

Someone asked me how she could take authority over her old nature. What an intriguing enigma this question presented! For years we've been told we have all authority in Jesus Christ, and we just need to take authority over our fears and our unbelief. First of all, have you ever thought where fear and unbelief reside? In your soul. Now, have you ever thought about which part of you "takes authority" over anything? Your soul.

Think about that for a minute. Remember when you have tried to tell your mind it was not afraid when it was? Remember when you have tried to tell your emotions they were not angry when they were? Remember when you have tried to reverse your will when it was in full "bull-in-a-china-shop" mode? All three parts of an unsurrendered soul are determined to think, feel, and do what they want. Your soul is not going to surrender its "authority" over any part of itself that it doesn't want to. And God won't take authority over any part of you that you have not surrendered to Him. So, what can you do? Bind your will to His will. The only real victory I've ever had with my stubborn, rebellious soul is to bind it to God's will and let Him work on it. Still, to my amazement. that very statement causes all kinds of negative reactions in and challenges from unsurrendered souls.

One of the main challenges I have received to using binding and loosing on unsurrendered souls is: People should not have to give up their "free will" in order to be in alignment with God's will. Today's Christians are very quick to defend their rights to exercise their free wills to make choices. God did say they could do that. But I made a free-will choice years ago to tell God I didn't want to exercise my so-called "free will" anymore—it wanted to choose too many things that caused me too much grief. I sense far more freedom within God's will for my life than I ever felt while I was fanning the "free will" flames of my soul.

The newspaper comics are frequently filled with all kinds of humorous inspiration for dealing with people today, especially the two strips named "B.C." and "Rose Is Rose." One other favorite of mine is "Cathy." One recent strip had Cathy shaking her fists in the air, demanding that her body quit producing fat. As a button popped defiantly off the waist of her pants, she said in defeat, "It's really tough to be the governing body when your body's doing the governing." Body or soul, Cathy expressed my sentiments exactly!

But I Just Don't Know What God Wants

God doesn't try to hide His precepts from us or make things difficult for us. He saw to it that everything we would ever need to know was recorded for all time and eternity in His Word for us to study and pray over. Our spirits are eager to respond to His will and His Word. Our souls are the part of us that always want to make Christianity seem so difficult. Our minds, wills, and emotions want to do an "end run" around the Cross of Calvary, looking for alternatives that will allow us a religion that requires no change, with all of change's seeming potential for price and pain. We so want to avoid any more pain, while we try to manage the pain we have with the latest fix-me-quick remedy on the self-help bookshelves.

The Scriptures tell us that we are to *"walk and live habitually in the (Holy Spirit)—responsive to and controlled and guided by the Spirit . . . "* (Gal. 5:16, AMP). An unsurrendered soul that is adamant about defending its right to free-will choice will never voluntarily surrender to being *"controlled by the* (Holy) *Spirit."* The unsurrendered soul will always be involved in a tug-of-war with the renewed part (spirit) of its human, tripartite being, as well as with the Holy Spirit. Obedience to this Scripture verse requires us to respond to this holy directive with completely surrendered <u>bodies, souls, and spirits</u> in order to be controlled and guided by God's Spirit.

That's easier than you think it is <u>when you have the master keys</u> to all the strait jackets, hand cuffs, bars, gates, and padlocked doors. But our unsurrendered souls don't want to do it the easy way. They want to do it the hard way—their way. When our souls won't surrender, God won't override them, but He may take us through some really hard things to show us that our own minds, wills, and emotions can't work the tough things out.

Still, if this can be accepted as encouragement, I believe that most who go through the hardest, most difficult times are the ones who are marked for the really great works of God. Such a glorious mark of greatness sometimes requires very intensive, hands-on, crash-dummy kinds of courses in Kingdom living. So, take heart if you are sincerely trying your best, but your life still seems like the war zones of Vietnam; you probably have the mark of real greatness upon your Christian destiny.

If you're in the middle of this kind of a war zone, seek out your most spiritually mature friends to pray with and speak truth to you, those you know who feed upon solid spiritual food and not just milk: *"Those whose senses and mental faculties are trained by practice to discriminate and distinguish between what is morally good and noble and what is evil and contrary either to divine or human law"* (Heb. 5:14, AMP).

Support, love, compassion, and caring are all part of the Christian's relationship to others. Sometimes support, love, and compassion are all that seems to be sustaining us when we are struggling with our unsurrendered souls, the devil, and the world. But we need to remember that the Word does not say that support, love, and compassion will ever set us free from our bondage. There are times when unconditional support and acceptance of "where we are" will only perpetuate our bondage. John 8:32 says that knowing the truth is what sets us free. Truth must be given with great love and much mercy, but truth must be given and received.

Those who are spiritually "unripe" or immature, having many unmet needs and unhealed hurts in their own souls, can pour much love and mercy out to those around them. This is because they quickly recognize and deeply empathize with the hurts and the needs of others. But these same compassionate believers are often incapable of balancing their love and mercy with pure truth. The one who loves best loves like Jesus did—with full grace and truth. (See John 1:14.)

Getting Close To God

Your soul is incredibly tricky, using many different approaches to keep you from dealing with the human reasoning and logic that stands between you and intimacy with God. When your soul can't get you to cast off all thoughts of God, it will deviously cooperate with what you think you can do for God. It will push you into great involvement in your church or your ministry, working to convince you that your fellowship with other Christians, your good deeds, your faithful church attendance, your tithes and offerings, your hours of service, are a reasonable substitute for intimate fellowship, prayer, and communion with God.

In the ministry, it is very easy to begin adding up all the hours you've spent preparing, preaching, and praying for people and mentally chalk that up to contributing to your personal relationship with God. But God is not interested in anything you do for Him if you're not interested in spending time with Him. Our soul can be glorying in what we are "doing" for God, while our spirit can be starving at the exact same time because of lack of intimacy with God.

In the original Greek, I find that Hebrews 12:1 has some interesting little nuances in it: *"Therefore, since we are surrounded by such a cloud of witnesses, let us throw off everything that hinders and the sin that so easily entangles, and let us run with perseverance the race marked out for us"* (NIV). The word *sin* used here comes from the Greek word *hamartia,* with a general definition meaning failing to hit the mark. We can be involved in so many things while running our own version of "the race," even good things which effectively entangle us in details that have nothing to do with <u>hitting the mark</u> of the high prize we are running for. *Entangled* or beset (KJV) in the original Greek means to be "thwarted, kept from running the race you are meant to run."

Take stock of your life. Perhaps you need to lay aside some relationships and involvements—things that may be <u>good but not God</u>. You may need to come apart from some of your Christian friends, interests, and activities to make time to concentrate solely on quality time with God. Do you remember the first time you fell in love or thought you did? You were willing to spend every available second being with or thinking about that person. Do you honestly feel that way about forsaking everything else to be <u>with</u> God?

Or, are you more interested in doing things <u>for</u> God? Our souls are always more interested in doing things "for God" because there can be praise and recognition from man for such acts. You must shut down the power drive of your own soul in order to become really intimate with God.

3

Satanic/Soulish Deception of the Church

I am very concerned with the church world's current interest in mixing worldly "conventional wisdom" with its doctrines of appropriate Christian ministry and counseling for the hurting and troubled. In trying to determine at what recent point the Christian church world became so enamored of psychotherapy techniques, I consulted the counseling section of a well-known, thirty-year-old book of Christian theology and read the following:

"Pastoral counseling represents a fusion of two not altogether discrete sources: pastoral care, i.e., the traditional shepherding function of the Christian minister and dynamic psychology, which focuses upon the striving aspects of personality as the key to understanding persons. Inasmuch as the latter has developed from the work of Sigmund Freud, counseling has seemed to be a concession to the enemy .... While this may be a source of difficulty to some Christian ministers, we seem to have reached a point where we recognize that all truth is God's truth . . . . The Christian who considers thoughtfully the findings of the psychotherapist sees many of the processes associated with the Christian's rebirth and sanctification operating in another context and described in a different vocabulary."

Good grief! No wonder we're in such a stew in the nineties if this is what some of our leaders have been learning for the last thirty years! The good news of the gospel remains very straightforward and simple. **Jesus has already done everything that needed to be done** in order to set us free from every ungodly thing we've ever done or had done to us. He opened the way for our spirits to be cleansed and restored to relationship with the Father's Spirit. We need to let go of the guilt, shame, anger, bitterness, and unforgiveness in our souls in order to make room to receive the full renewal and blessings of all the rights of that relationship.

We desperately need to understand that <u>Jesus really wants us free</u>. I spoke with one minister regarding using the keys of binding and loosing to open up areas of our souls to God's grace and deliverance. This leader became quite excited and exclaimed, "I get it! Then the hurts won't hurt as much anymore." I replied that Jesus didn't want us to learn to live with less internal pain, but to be set completely free from it.

"Then what happens is we will be strong enough to deal with the hurt," the minister said. I replied that the answer was not learning to be strong enough to deal with hurt, but learning to surrender enough to let His grace heal the hurt. We went through several other variations on this theme—being able to forget the hurt, becoming stronger than the hurt, being able to forgive the hurt, etc. This person found it incredibly difficult to grasp that the power of the hurt could really be neutralized by God's grace. We've been taught far too much about processes, programs, and steps to employ in learning how to deal with our pain. As a result, we have not pursued understanding how to open ourselves up to God's healing grace.

Artificial Life Support

Our pain is kept alive by the artificial life support systems of our unrenewed minds, wills, and emotions. As long as our souls can convince us that they must be included in our healing process, they dictate the terms of the healing. Our souls reinforce their emotional leverage for accomplishing this by a continual infusing of "artificial life" into our painful memories.

Your unsurrendered soul has kept records of everything that has ever been done to, said to, or taken away from you. It believes that the answers to resolving these injustices all reside in facts that are stored in your memory; all it must do is find the right facts to process. This is why every new self-help book or program about self-empowerment intrigues the untransformed mind. People think, "Maybe this one will put everything together for me to finally make sense of my life."

Digging up and prioritizing the who and the what of your past is not the answer. God's healing work of grace has nothing to do with who is to blame for anything—someone else or yourself. Divine grace simply requires you to disengage your soul's fixation on all of the unresolved issues and blame placing out of your past, and do what God says. Grace will not only enable you to do this, grace will also fix everything else that seems so painfully impossible.

This is beyond the understanding of the unsurrendered soul. The natural, carnal, untransformed mind or old nature of the believer does not, indeed cannot, understand anything of the ways of the Spirit of God. Because it is at enmity with and hostile to God (see Rom. 8:7) and His divine ways, it will fight every step you make towards God unless you disable its power to alarm and intimidate you with fear tactics.

Just Give It Up

What do you do when the old "stuff" in your trash can under your sink is overflowing with wet, smelly garbage? Do you buy books to understand the process of removing it? Do you get together with others who have the same kind of garbage under their sink and talk about it? Do you join a group to help you learn the twelve steps of trash removal? Do you pick through it to try to analyze who is responsible for putting the coffee grounds, the egg shells, the tin cans, in there? No! You throw it out. End of garbage, end of subject. There is a distinct similarity here to what we need to do with the baggage from our past, although the mode of operation is a little different.

Binding and loosing prayers stabilize and steady you while empowering you to let the Holy Spirit go deep within your soul to neutralize all of your painful memories and file them as neutered facts. This is not some form of holy amnesia or self-denial. The facts of any trauma you've sustained will still exist, but they will be stripped of all the pain you've learned to associate with them. They will become <u>neutral memories</u>. Your part is to tear down your self-protective walls to expose your soul's control over the artificial life of your past. Then the Holy Spirit can take over and fix **any** problem you have ever been able to get yourself into.

God never intended that becoming strong, useful, productive Christians would be all that hard. Honest! We don't have to stop bullets with our hand, leap tall buildings with a single jump, or step in front of speeding trains. We just have to come to a place of <u>active agreement with</u> and then <u>act on</u> God's precepts, whether we understand them or not.

You don't have to understand a carburetor in order to drive a car; you don't have to understand electricity in order to turn on a light. Trust scriptural precepts and principles to work because God said they will. Stop building protective strongholds around erroneous, worldly principles that don't work, never have worked, and never will work for you. Stop strengthening your soul's power to continue to confuse and deceive you by blocking out the only thing that never fails—God's truth.

Here a Spirit, There a Spirit

Christians are prone in these days to label far too many things as "evil spirits." One Bible teacher said a certain lady had a "Doris Day spirit." I hadn't heard that one, but I have heard over and over about controlling spirits, unteachable spirits, Jezebel spirits, etc.—none of which exist! That which you think is a "controlling spirit" is a frightened, angry person whose soul is trying to control his life and anyone else's who gets too close for comfort. That which you think is an "unteachable spirit" is an unteachable soul that is terrified that it doesn't have all the answers and can be tricked by someone else's smooth talking. That which is labeled a "Jezebel spirit" is a person with a devious, manipulative, strong-willed soul. The label of "Jezebel spirit" is also used both to "mark" and diminish many in the Church today who are over-zealous in seeking position and attention. This carnality is not the work of an evil spirit, rather it is wrong behaviors driven by powerful unmet needs deep within an unsurrendered soul.

Why has there been so much focus on evil spirits instead of the unsurrendered soul? For one thing, our souls shrink from personal responsibility and accountability for anything that has to do with our strongest fears and most embarrassing failures. But, if what is wrong with us is the work of an evil spirit, then it is not really our fault. There is always the hope that we can go to a deliverance ministry and get it cast out of us. There is one big problem with this misplaced hopefulness: *You cannot be delivered from yourself!*

We have chosen to throw ourselves into wrong spiritual fights because there are more books, tapes, mentors, and ministries dealing with the realm of demons than with the soulish realm. We feel more support from the Christian community in fighting with evil spirits than with our own souls, because everyone has been told that we have all power and authority over evil spirits. So, it appears logical to fight what we are being told we can beat. This is the same skewed logic as the joke about the person who was searching diligently under a bright street light, around midnight, for a lost wallet. Questioned about where the wallet may have been dropped, the person replied, "Over there in that vacant lot." When asked why he wasn't searching in the vacant lot, he said, "It's too dark over there, but I can see fine here."

Many are willing to train you to fight the fight they believe you can win—the battle with your external enemy—an already defeated foe. Few today have been telling you how to win the battle with your internal foe, your unsurrendered soul, because they aren't sure if you really can.

How We Have Missed the Truth

Another reason Christians have created so many doctrines about evil spirits is a superficial identification with the word "spirit" as it is used in the Old Testament. I am not a Hebrew scholar by any means, but it does not take a master's degree to do a little Hebrew research in a good lexicon. For purposes of research, I generally start in my *Strong's Hebrew and Chaldee Dictionary* and my *Gesenius' Hebrew-Chaldee Lexicon to the Old Testament.* Even I can get around in these two reference books.

Psalms 51:16-17 (KJV) is an interesting place to begin: *"For thou desirest not sacrifice; else would I give it: thou delightest not in burnt offering. The sacrifices of God are a broken spirit; a broken and a contrite heart, O God, thou wilt not despise."* I always struggled with this verse, asking, "God, why do you want to break my spirit? This is probably the only part of me that is right."

The word spirit here comes from the Hebrew word *ruwach,* which has several variations of meaning. *Gesenius* 7307 (3a), translates *ruwach* here as meaning "the rational mind or spirit, the seat of the senses, affections, and emotions of various kinds." This is obviously man's soul, his mind and emotions. In other words, a broken and submissive soul is an acceptable sacrifice to God. The word heart in this verse comes from the Hebrew word *lebab* 3824 (a,b), which *Gesenius* describes as "the soul, life, the seat of the senses, affections, and emotions of the mind." This is closely related to the Hebrew word *leb* 3820, which Strong describes as the feelings, the will, and even the intellect."

I had always assumed that the word contrite in this verse meant sorry or sorrowful, i.e., a repentant heart. The Hebrew meaning for the word that the King James Version translates here as contrite, *dakah* 1794, is "to collapse, to be broken to pieces, to be crushed." So, this reference to the contrite heart means a broken and crushed soul. (Refer back to The Bridge at the beginning of the book for definitions of the Greek word for loose, *luo*, meaning shattered, broken, smashed, etc.) I believe it also perfectly describes a soul that has experienced a loosing, tearing down, and shattering of its strongholds, excuses, self-protection mechanisms, etc.

Eugene Peterson says it very well in *The Message* (Psalm 51:16-17), *"Going through the motions doesn't please you, a flawless performance is nothing to you. I learned God-worship when my pride was shattered. Heart-shattered lives ready for love don't for a moment escape God's notice."*

Isaiah 61:3 (KJV) refers to a spirit of heaviness. The New International Version has translated this as a spirit of despair. The Amplified Bible translates this as a heavy, burdened, and failing spirit. The word "spirit" here is once again the Hebrew word *ruwach* meaning the rational mind or spirit, the seat of the senses, affections, and emotions of various kinds. This verse is not describing a troubling spirit, it is describing an inward attitude of the soul of man. With regard to this particular verse, *Gesenius* also refers to fear in the emotional part of the soul.

Proverbs 25:28 (KJV) tells us that he who has no rule over his own spirit is like a city that is broken down and without walls. Once again, this is the Hebrew word *ruwach,* rendered as meaning the seat of the senses, affections and emotions of various kinds. He who has no rule over his own soul is like a city that is broken down and without walls. Isaiah 19:14 (KJV) speaks of a perverse spirit, which *Gesenius* says is the rendering of *ruwach* 7307 (b) to mean a mode of thinking and acting, the implication being that of a perverse mind and its ensuing actions. Hosea 4:12 (KJV) speaks of the spirit of whoredoms. The word spirit here means a "disposition common to many, or a mode of thinking and acting" *Gesenius* 7037 (b).

Many evil "spirits" spoken of in the church world today cannot be found anywhere in the Bible as actual entities: spirit of rebellion, spirit of rejection, spirit of unbelief, controlling spirit, grieving spirit, victim spirit, Jezebel spirit, spirit of lust, religious spirit, etc. All of these descriptive adjectives used to identify and name so-called evil "spirits" are **attitudes of the unsurrendered soul**. How much more productive our spiritual dealings will be when we focus our warfare on the right sources of our problems.

The above examples are certainly not intended to be considered as being a definitive and final word study on "spirits." These explanations are meant only to show how we have accepted so many erroneous premises as the foundation of so much of our spiritual warfare. Evil spirits do exist, probably everywhere, and they are very dangerous. But a washed-in-the-blood, born-again, forgiven believer does not have to war with them <u>for the working out of his own salvation</u>. The working out of your own salvation as described in Philippians 2:12 is referring to bringing your unsurrendered soul into alignment with God's will and purposes. The believer's strength lies in using scriptural truth to close all <u>doors of access</u> (created in and by the soul of man) to evil spirits without.

Use the truth in Matthew 16:19 and begin loosing deception, denial, strongholds, wrong beliefs, and wrong agreements from your soul. This will help you to close doors of access for personal attack from evil spirits and neutralize your unsurrendered soul's attempts to hinder your regenerated spirit's gift of discernment. These are the first steps in identifying and dispatching wrong spirits working within a believer's sphere of influence! Evil spirits will be drawn to any area of vulnerability in your soul. When open doors of access are available, wrong spirits will be drawn right to them to do their dirty work. All existing problems of the unsurrendered soul are then compounded. Don't let this happen to you.

There Are Genuine Evil Spirits

There are specifically named demonic spirits, but they are far fewer than what is generally believed. The Bible names one of them as a <u>familiar spirit</u> (Lev. 20:27), referring to a soothsaying demon. Many have believed the two references in the Old Testament (1 Kings 22:22-23, and 2 Chron. 18:21-22) of a <u>lying spirit</u> validated the existence of a demon of lying. I find these references extremely interesting, but unsupportive of such a belief. In these passages, the prophet Micaiah envisioned the Lord sitting on His throne with the host of heaven standing around Him. In 1 Kings 22:20-22 (NIV) the Lord said to angels, *"'Who will entice Ahab into attacking Ramoth Gilead and going to his death there?' One suggested this, and another that. Finally, a spirit came forward, stood before the Lord and said, 'I will entice him ... I will go out and be a lying spirit in the mouths of all his prophets.'"* The Lord told the spirit to go and do it. It did, and Ahab went to battle and was killed.

I used to wonder if this refers to one of God's holy angels who agreed to be a lying spirit, or an evil spirit ordered to do God's bidding. What I now find most interesting is that *Gesenius* states that the word "spirit," again a variation of the Hebrew word *ruwach* 7307 (4), in these passages refers to the personification of the prophetic Spirit.

Baker's 1979 edition of *The Gesenius Old Testament Lexicon* lists a disclaimer here that says this "must be taken as a defective designation of the Holy Ghost," (i.e., that it is not the Holy Ghost). Frankly, I'm still chewing on this one!

1 Samuel 16:14 (KJV) says, *"But the spirit of the Lord departed from Saul, and an evil spirit from the Lord troubled him."* I've heard all kinds of doctrinal gymnastics trying to explain this one away. Both uses of the word spirit in this verse come from the Hebrew word *ruwach,* which I believe basically is describing God's breath or wind, His Spirit, life, or the soul of man. God will use what we may consider as "bad" or "good" and bring His desired will and purposes out of either one.

51

This has never been a problem to me, for I believe that God knows what He's doing at all times and frequently I don't. But, hallelujah, Romans 8:28 says that *"all things work together for good"* in the lives of those who love God and are called according to His purposes. God is never out of control of **anything, anywhere, anytime!**

So, if you're thoroughly confused at this point, let me go back to my original stated purpose for the above (limited) word study on "spirits." I want to show that **a superficial acceptance of certain words in the Bible has caused many to build an entire structure of spiritual warfare based upon false premises.** This explains why we seemingly have so much spiritual knowledge available to us these days without a corresponding ratio of consistent spiritual victory in the Body of Christ.

Spiritual or Secular Psychology?

I am occasionally confronted with my previous writings and statements that have been somewhat negative about Christian support groups, twelve-step programs, and some forms of spiritual counseling. That's just one problem with writing strong statements and then having them reproduced thousands of times in books with your name on them. Smarter people than me have known this longer than I have and often avoid saying very controversial things just for that reason. This may be smarter, but it can also result in withheld truth.

In the last year I have been firmly confronted by well-meaning Christian leaders and professionals regarding my positions on three of the counterfeit "manifestations" of the unsurrendered soul, i.e., the wounded inner child, the multiple personality disorder, and the repressed memory syndrome. I have been advised by others in the ministry to be quiet about these issues and let the flak die down. I have tried to, but something cries out in me every time I hear a Christian's damaged soul justifying that believer's acceptance of enormous self-limitations because of some psychological explanation and validation of a victim mentality.

The church world today has found itself without answers to many deeply troubling issues of mental and emotional disorders, having seemingly tried all of the principles being taught in today's Bible schools and seminaries. Deliverance practices of casting out evil spirits have not produced permanent healing in many who have sought answers there. Specialized groups and programs have not consistently produced permanent healing in those who have sought help there. Out of frustration and perhaps desperation, some Christian training institutes, as well as practicing Christian counselors and therapists, have sought to integrate their therapy techniques with some of the latest findings from secular psychological sources. This has rarely been a spiritually productive union, but instead has bolstered the soul's position as the gatekeeper to the source of the problem.

Repressed Memory Syndrome

Some pastors and Christian counselors are now being sued for "spiritual" counseling gone awry. We must not paint all such backlashes as works of the devil or ungodly attacks from the world. There have been many recorded instances of Christian counselors using techniques designed to "uncover" repressed memories of satanic ritual abuse, parental sexual abuse, or other forms of abuse to explain why certain clients have not been healed. I recently read of one such case in the nation's courts where a Christian counselor helped a young Christian woman "recover a repressed memory" of her minister father impregnating her by rape and then inducing an abortion of the fetus with a coat hanger. It was later medically documented that the young woman was a virgin, and the father had received a vasectomy many years prior to the supposed abuse. This family has been ripped to pieces because of the deception potential in the secular "memory recovery" counseling technique used by a Christian counselor.

This particular psychological deception (repressed memory syndrome) seems to appeal to the souls of both males and females, although the majority of the cases I have heard of seem to be women. The following two psychological deceptions, however, seem to be embraced mostly by the female wounded soul.

Multiple Personality Disorder

I have prayed with and ministered to believers who have been told that their seemingly unsolvable mental and emotional problems stem from a "multiple personality disorder." I believe the latest term for this is disassociative disorder, however, I do not try to keep up on the changing labels. Recently, in a fairly large meeting, I was ministering to a woman displaying the symptoms of this "disorder," following an hour of teaching on binding and loosing to dismantle the unsurrendered soul's control. Several present, who knew her, wanted to help by giving me the name of the "dominant" personality who would be most cooperative with my ministering.

I politely and firmly turned down such information, refusing to give credibility to the separate counterfeit "personalities" of this desperately troubled, wounded, and fragmented soul. I continued, in prayer, to bind the fragmented soul (as a single entity) to God's will and purposes, to the truth, and to the mind of Christ. After much initial nonsense and reacting from the soul that was used to having its masquerade defense mechanism accepted, I was finally able to talk calmly and lovingly to this person as a singular presence. We will never achieve permanent solutions and healing for wounded souls by naming, speaking to, and giving credibility to the masquerades being perpetrated from within the soul itself!

Wounded Inner Child

The "wounded inner child" theory is a devastating deception that allows hurting, desperate, controlling souls to retreat behind a cloak of childishness. Those who believe they have an inner victim/child suffer from perceived rejection, betrayal, fright, and pain that is believed to be coming from deliberate acts of others who have no intent to hurt at all. I am amazed at how many individuals today excuse fears, self-limitations, wrong behaviors, and inordinately sensitive "feelings" by claiming to have a "wounded inner child."

I remember observing one woman who had lived with hurt feelings, wrong patterns of thinking, and great pain for some time. She had been through many years of Christian counseling, part of which was addressed to her "wounded inner child." I was unsure whether or not an opposing viewpoint of ministry would be received, but God has His perfect timing. One day this woman agreed to renounce and loose all wrong agreements with the "wounded inner child" theory, as well as all victim mentality programming. Then she repented to the Lord for having believed it in the first place. We prayed and bound her will to the will of God, her mind to the mind of Christ, and every facet of her being—body, soul, and spirit—to the truth of the Word.

I did not speak with this woman again until months later, shortly after a major family get together in her home. This woman had always worked extremely hard to make all family meetings the perfect experience she had never known as a child. When others seemed to overlook and ignore the enormous effort she put into such gatherings, she was always crushed. Retreating behind hurt feelings and suppressed anger, old family dynamics would take over and everyone would begin to revert to old patterns of conflict.

This holiday, however, a major victory had come. The woman was no longer desperately trying to single-handedly create the perfect holiday environment/family experience that her "inner child" had always dreamed of. She approached the whole family experience with no preconceived expectations—positive or negative. God filled her with His grace to rejoice in what was good, ignore what might have turned to bad, and a wonderful time was had by all.

I am well aware that isolated testimonies do not validate spiritual theories. So, I continued to struggle for some kind of verification that there was something very wrong with Christian counseling that was relying upon false, secular, psychological premises. Without any technical, medical, or theological support for my beliefs on this subject (other than there being no scriptural validation of any of these so-called disorders), I admit I felt a concern over my lack of proof.

The Secular World's Victim Manufacturing Industry

Just days before submitting the final draft of this book to my editor, I found an obscure reference on the Internet to a new secular book from Canada called *Manufacturing Victims,* written by Dr. Tana Dineen. I felt a quickening in my spirit and managed to locate and order a copy of this book for overnight delivery to my office.

In this book, the very credible Dr. Dineen tells how she was drawn to the study of psychology in 1965, completing an honours bachelor of science degree (1969), with a masters (1971) and a doctoral degree (1975) in psychology. She was licensed as a psychologist in both Ontario and British Columbia. By 1993, she felt that psychology had become an "industry" in which many of her colleagues were creating "users" and manufacturing "victims." She left her clinical practice and began to research and write an expose on the current practices of the psychological field.

Dr. Dineen and I had a very interesting conversation via e-mail, and she stated that she had great respect for those who were devoted to helping people spiritually. Her only problem with religious "counselors" came when they tried to incorporate secular psychological jargon into their spiritual doctrines. I heartily agree with and highly endorse this observation.

One of secular psychology's own authorities has stepped forward and decried the self-serving practices of the many who have encouraged victim-manufacturing techniques. These "counseling" techniques fit over the masquerades of the unsurrendered soul like a kid glove.

How long I have waited for someone more "qualified" experientially and educationally than I to say these practices were dangerous and dead wrong. I encourage anyone who is involved in giving or receiving therapy to get a copy of Dr. Dineen's book, *Manufacturing Victims,* for further understanding.

The Church must return to its roots of using spiritual truth, mixed with love, mercy, grace, and compassion, to minister to those who are confused and hurting. We must turn away from all of the false premises of secular psychology and teach our own wounded that the truth of Christ's completed work and the grace of God are the only sources of healing and wholeness. The unsurrendered soul within believers must be made to surrender all of its self-contrived defense systems to allow the infusion of this loving, healing truth of grace.

2 Corinthians 10:4-5 (AMP) tells us that *"the weapons of our warfare are not physical (weapons of flesh and blood), but they are mighty before God for the overthrow and destruction of strongholds, [inasmuch as we] refute arguments and theories and reasonings and every proud and lofty thing that sets itself up against the (true) knowledge of God...."* Our God-given weapons are for the destruction and overthrow of our souls' arguments and theories and reasonings, as well as any humanistic theories of the world's "healers"—every proud and lofty thing that would set itself up in our minds to keep us from really knowing God. Answers to healing for the pain, anger, and fear of unsurrendered souls will never come from carnal, human avenues of help—psychiatrists, gurus, the government, the judicial systems, educational systems, or anything else—only from God.

Formula Answers, No Answers or Wrong Answers

Because of little or no understanding of the sources of the drives that cause the manifestation of wrong behaviors, many ministers and leaders who are asked for counsel give formula answers, no answers, or wrong answers. I know one married minister who struggled with homosexual thoughts for years after leaving a lifetime of that lifestyle. One of his greatest frustrations was that he knew he must stop "being" homosexual, but no one could tell him how to begin "being" heterosexual. He felt like the house had been swept clean with no furniture or occupants in it, simply waiting for demons to eventually return and find it empty. God's healing grace can seem totally abstract to those who are still enshrouded in grave clothes from their pasts.

This born-again minister went to at least six pastors and spiritual leaders, forcing himself to be painfully transparent before them in an attempt to receive help that no one knew how to give. I do believe a struggling "homosexual" man or woman can be a born-again Christian. Your spiritual position as a member of God's family, once you have accepted Jesus Christ as your Savior, is not invalidated by behaviors you're struggling to overcome. It is not true that the validity of our salvation experience can be "determined" by human judgment calls on wrong behaviors we have not yet overcome.

When this born-again minister went for counsel, each of these leaders honestly confessed he did not know the answer to the man's struggle, but they all promised they would pray. Prayer is <u>never</u> wrong. But when faith-filled prayer is knit together with words of compassion and hope, specific scriptural guidelines on how to reach root causes of wrong behaviors, along with words of practical wisdom, a spiritual safety net is created to catch one who is falling deeper into hopelessness.

So Many Trials and Tribulations

Believers who are constantly struggling and torn between having one hand wrapped tightly in the hem of Jesus' garment while the other hand is desperately holding on to familiar behavioral crutches of the world, usually have two factors present in their lives: 1) They don't know how to cooperate with God, therefore, they're living out their Christianity the toughest way possible; and 2) They have a potential for becoming fearless defenders of the faith once they eventually emerge from the refining fire. When the Holy Spirit is finally able to bring them through all of the fiery trials and tribulations needed to burn away their dross and cement their faith and trust in God, they will be ready for supernatural spiritual assignments that will give the devil and his demons heart attacks.

It is sad, however, when trials and tribulations cause some believers to feel persecuted and overwhelmed with what they perceive as God having let them down. Think for a moment about those believers you've heard other people say this about: "Oh, he's just been so wounded. Why, he's had so many hard things happen. It's amazing that he is still in the ministry—or in the church—or married—or whatever. That poor, poor, dear man," or "that poor, poor, dear woman."

To generate that kind of sympathy and talk, you can almost guarantee this person has spoken fairly often to others about his or her wounds. There is nothing wrong with wanting someone to pray with you, listen to you, and help you through a hard time. But some "saints"—who are just "carrying their cross and bearing their God-given burden of life" (also known as being on the Potter's wheel!)—adopt a victim mentality they then use to gently manipulate others. These people feel safest when they know you are aware of all they have "suffered," when they know you are aware of their limitations because of what they've been through.

On the other side of this coin are the people who, even though they have been through seemingly terrible trials and loss, are so secure in their faith and trust in God that it's hard to believe that anything bad has ever happened to them. No victim mentality here! No one says, "Oh, that poor woman," or "that poor, poor man," about them. People only marvel at their strength and their faith and their power and their authority in Christ Jesus. People are drawn to them because of the life and the light that sparks off them like they are under an arc welder.

You can learn to cooperate with God and speed up your process of getting there. Bind your will to the will of God, and bind your mind to the mind of Christ. Begin to loose the strongholds and other power tactics of your soul and choke off its whining about the unfairness of life whenever things start nipping into your comfort zone. This form of praying is not to get what you want—rather to bring into being what your heavenly Father wants. Through binding and loosing prayers, by the words of your mouth, loose all of the wrong attitudes and mind-sets that have kept you from surrendering to the full process of God's workbench because of your deepest fears and oldest pain.

61

He Must Increase, I Must Decrease

The key to moving into everything God has for us—
healing, revelation knowledge, the ability to work
miracles, all the Word promises to each believer—keeps
coming back to one thing. This is the same thing that
good preachers have been saying ever since John the
Baptist said it: *"He must increase, but I must decrease"*
(John 3:30, KJV). The "I" here is the same for him, me
and you—our unsurrendered souls. The basic laws of
physics tell us that two things cannot occupy the same
space, i.e., the same throne, at the same time. Your
unsurrendered soul's territorial rights to running any part
of your life must decrease, ultimately disappearing, before
He can increase in you.

There really is nothing new under the sun; the perfect
solutions to every problem or circumstance have always
been right there in the Word. Whenever someone comes
along with something that seems fresh and new from God,
it's just another facet in one of God's existing diamonds
of truth. But we don't always recognize new facets of
revelation from Him, rejecting them if we can't
superimpose our single facet of truth on them.

"Well," you might say, "I just don't understand how
this binding and loosing is going to help me get over all
the things I've been through, or I'm going through now.
I've been hurt so much. I'm not a strong Christian, I'm
not even a very brave person. I'm really quite hesitant to
do anything that might make the devil mad." Well, take
heart, "little sheep." You don't have to do anything but
dismantle the power structure of your own soul and then
listen to what will begin to flow from your spirit. Surely
you're not afraid of your own soul—your mind, will,

and emotions? You've listened to your soul, walked with it, talked with it, and conversed with it since you were born. You've probably also turned over the reins of your life to it, as well.

Perhaps you have some pretty solid ideas about what you've already been taught regarding your soul, personal strongholds, and binding and loosing. You probably have your own way of praying and enacting spiritual warfare, and your way may have helped you to build some front-line defenses. But has your way focused on dealing with the ongoing manipulation and hindrances of your unsurrendered soul, itself? The last thing you need in these last days is an internal "foe" using areas of your own vulnerability to manipulate whatever choices you make.

We can be so deceived as we labor to protect ourselves from what we perceive to be our external enemies. We build elaborate, self-constructed defense mechanisms (strongholds) out of misplaced trust in our own ability to recognize danger and then make right choices about it. Isaiah 57:10 (AMP) is a perfect picture of what all of us have tried to do on our own, *"You were wearied with the length of your way [in trying to find rest and satisfaction in alliances apart from the true God]; yet you did not say, There is no result or profit. You found quickened strength, therefore you were not faint or heartsick [or penitent]."*

We are such short-sighted, finite-minded little creatures. Here we have become equal partners in the biggest, can't-lose, "family" operation of all time and eternity, and we feel we need to fight an already defeated devil in order to maintain and/or improve our position in this family. We believe God needs us to push back the darkness and pull down the devil's schemes. May this book reveal truth to you in such a way that it will set you free from all of the entrapment of this soulish and satanic scam.

God Does Do Roadblocks

Your soul, if left unchallenged, can exert so much pressure upon you that you will even fight a roadblock of the Holy Spirit, believing that it is Satan who is preventing you from having something. This is a very dangerous error. Authorities generally set up roadblocks to stop people from driving vehicles into dangerous or unsafe circumstances. I believe God does the same thing. But there are times when we **do not** or **do not want to** recognize one of His roadblocks. So we land in the canyon. (Please forgive an irresistible mixed metaphor here, out of Chapter 2, but we can also end up shipwrecking ourselves on a rocky coast or ramming into a lighthouse!).

We must begin to see God as the Almighty One in control of all aspects of every circumstance, rather than just being the "tow truck" we call to get us out of the canyon. We must let God be God, for He is good. He knows what is best for us. We have a sure word of this in Jeremiah 29:11 (NIV), *"'I know the plans I have for you,' declares the Lord, 'plans to prosper you and not to harm you, plans to give you hope and a future.'"*

Hallelujah!

4

Wrong Behaviors, Word Curses, and Generational Bondages

At first, my lack of formal psychological training was a source of distress to me as I began to recognize the extent of the emotional baggage that many Christians carry. I have had battered Christians, Christian batterers, Christians with frozen emotions, Christians with great fear, Christians with control issues, dishonest Christians, and Christians with sexual perversions come to me and confess incredible things. These believers were trying to serve Jesus while packing hundreds of pounds of stinking garbage on their shoulders. I was deeply concerned to realize I knew very little about some of the issues they brought up.

Gradually I realized that I don't need intensive training in every kind of hellish thing people are struggling with, because only the Holy Spirit knows exactly how to fix them all. The church world today too often chooses to employ the world's conventional wisdom on counseling to try to fine tune and tailor God's healing and deliverance. This does not interest God a bit. He doesn't use multiple steps, specialized counseling, or problem-specific therapy when He sets people free. He just knocks on the door of their frightened souls' defense systems and asks, *"Are you ready yet, my child?"*

I believe God wants every frightened, hurting lamb who feels hopelessly entangled in sin and wrong behaviors to know what I believe to be His heart's message: *"Tear down your stronghold walls, cast down your vain imaginations and anything else you've let be exalted between you and me, so you can know me. Let my grace and truth and mercy come into your hidden areas of shame, need, and pain—and heal you. Know me and know my truth, for it and my unfailing love will set you free."* God's Word covers every kind of unmet need, every unresolved issue, and every unhealed hurt. (See John 1:14, 17; 2 Cor. 10:4-5; John 8:32.)

How The Church Views Wrong Behavior

Teaching Christians how to conduct themselves in a godly manner is a worthwhile, spiritually correct endeavor. But when this endeavor is not balanced with spiritual understanding, grace, and life, legalism begins to creep into the teachings. Christians who have never been taught to understand the <u>true</u> source of their unacceptable behaviors and the power of their unmet needs can fail miserably in overcoming them. Discouraged, these believers finally just try to hide what they can't conquer. This is especially true if they have attained a reputation of being a "good Christian," and fear being exposed as a hypocrite. They begin living a double life, having a double mind, being doubly miserable.

We must teach all Christians to make room within their souls to receive grace, truth, and life, *"Christ in you, the* [only] *hope of glory"* (Col. 1:27, KJV, author's [only]). His life in us truly is our only hope of permanently changing the reaping cycle of the bad fruit that results from the wrong behaviors we can't seem to escape. Most Christians can modify some of their wrong behaviors, disguise them, and even temporarily bury some of them. But this is only a "front line" defense measure. When you have unmet needs deep in your soul that are continually pushing for resolution, the force of those drives will eventually surface when you least expect it. The answer is not to get your problems under "your control," but to have your internal sources of those problems healed by the grace of God.

Most Christians try to crucify their flesh by changing their external behaviors—and such self-denial is not a bad thing. Self-denial can be a noble attempt to obey God, but it is not a permanent solution. It is an effort of the will that can wear you out if you have inner drives continually sabotaging your efforts. Most new Christians make a fairly serious attempt to stop drinking, smoking, cursing, gambling, doing drugs, fornication, to name a few of the most obvious things a new Christian learns to let go of. But such accomplishments are often only modifications of external behavior manifestations attained through sheer willpower.

If a change in behavior comes only from a soul's decision that there is a benefit to a more "appropriate" external behavior manifestation—i.e., social acceptance, church standing, image enhancement—it will often work towards achieving that goal. However, any change in circumstances that brings about a termination of the benefit will likely change the soul's determination of appropriate behavior as well. A change in circumstances will not alter behavior issuing from a surrendered soul that has learned to receive God's grace and mercy.

Outward Behaviors Have Inward Sources

No one, either devil or human, can get a Christian to do any wrong thing he doesn't already have an inward source driving him towards. The initial source of our most ungodly drives is not Satan, contrary to the popular belief of much of the church world. However, the devil will do everything he can to help us destroy ourselves in our self-efforts to control our inner drives, meet our own needs, and quiet our own pain. He will manipulate others who have the same needs to tempt us, and he will manipulate self-righteous Christians to damn us.

If no light of understanding and hope is held aloft to guide, very needy people can and will lead other needy people into dangerous territory. Those who are already in wrong lifestyles often introduce new participants into the same lifestyles—adultery, drug use, sexual perversion, stealing, etc. When a self-destructive behavior produces temporary relief from your unmet needs, the one thing that can temporarily lighten the load of related pain and shame is to have someone else under it with you.

But, Jesus Christ within us cleanses us, gives us a new nature, and a solid-gold "second" chance to be everything we were created to be, no matter how low we've fallen. He has already done everything to ensure our ability to rise up and overcome all things. Our part is to take the keys He has provided for us and strip the power sources of our old natures that riddle us with guilt, doubt, and conflict of faith, which are smoke screens designed to cloud our understanding that all of His promises are for us, too. Any Christian who has the right "keys," and knows how to use them, can receive divine empowerment to walk in full freedom.

Our wrong behaviors generally began as we learned that certain behaviors seemed to help us "cope" with our unmet needs, unhealed hurts, and unresolved issues. Contrary to the church world's conventional wisdom, I believe homosexual and lesbian lifestyles begin from misguided self-attempts to meet unmet needs. Someone in the homosexual lifestyle was present at just the "right time" to reach out and comfort someone else whose unmet needs were overwhelming. Because homosexuality is disobedience to God, this requires a man or woman to automatically feel the need to justify and rationalize the behavior. This rationalization and justification process (building of strongholds) opens the door to evil spirits who torment and tempt the individual to move deeper into the sin.

When we repeatedly give the devil room, footholds, and opportunities in our lives (Eph. 4:27, AMP) through the presence of personal strongholds, we find ourselves in double trouble with our misery and desperation intensified. Our sinful "coping" behaviors end up being driven by two sources: 1) Our unmet needs, unresolved issues, and unhealed hurts that are demanding relief and/ or gratification; and 2) Torment and pressure from unclean spirits.

You must dismantle your soul's strongholds to give the Holy Spirit entrance into every area of your soul. This is your part. The Holy Spirit does the rest.

Natural Strategies Won't Win Spiritual Fights

Christ's life received is the beginning of permanent freedom. His life flowing into our lives causes many wrong behaviors to fall away and evil spirits to run away. But when religious rules and regulations alone are imparted to the soul, wrong behaviors are only modified or temporarily corralled, and evil spirits patiently wait nearby. Christian behavior modification does not change the wrong behaviors, it only repositions them.

For example, years ago, Christian men were told to always avert their eyes from attractive women so lust could not come in through the "eye-gates" of their souls. This, in effect, meant the only safe female was an "ugly" female. Not a very Christian-like or practical solution. Averting one's eyes is a form of behavior modification, not a means of enforcing pure thinking. You cannot enforce pure thinking, you can only think pure thoughts.

This is not double talk. This is knowing how to move your thought processes out of the realm of your soul's control and into Christ-like thinking. This is accomplished by *"bringing every thought into captivity to Christ,"* as commanded in 2 Corinthians 10:5. The instructions immediately preceding this commandment clearly define the "how" part: *"The weapons of our warfare are not carnal, but mighty through God to the pulling down of strong holds; casting down imaginations* [Greek: ideas], *and every high thing that exalteth itself against the knowledge of God....* " (2 Cor. 10:4-5, KJV). Using the Kingdom key of loosing in prayer always helps me recognize wrong ideas and thought patterns coming into my mind. Then I have to choose to bind my mind to the mind of Christ and loose the wrong thought patterns I have identified.

Coping Techniques

Modifying a wrong behavior, regardless of good intent, simply helps you substitute a secondary coping behavior to get past the source of the problem one more time. Coping techniques work primarily only by the grace of God, and secondarily because the enemy's focus is on other areas of your life. When the enemy moves toward an area of your life that you are controlling with a coping behavior, and God lifts His grace to allow it (and He will if you have repeatedly refused to let Him into the source of the need), you will be in for a rough ride. Satan will turn the heat up on you in that area until you are dangerously surrounded by many forms of temptation. He is not called "the prince of this world" for nothing, for he is fully able to maneuver worldly things, wrong people, dangerous opportunities, and soulish as well as physical pressures into your path.

When coping behaviors are your means of resisting external temptations, you will increase your dependency upon and frequency of using them—always in direct conflict with your faith and trust in God. Defense mechanisms in your soul stand between you and God, a direct disobedience that gives Satan legal right to harass you. This is a very bad place for a Christian to be! Surrendering your defense mechanisms and your fears to God to allow Him into those scary, dark areas where even you've been afraid to go, is a very good place to be. It is the second smartest choice you will ever make— accepting Jesus Christ as your Savior was the first, of course. Only He can permanently deliver your new creature from the influence of your old man.

Heritage Hindrances

The Bible says in Isaiah 54:17, *"No weapon that is formed against thee shall prosper; and every tongue that shall rise against thee in judgment thou shalt condemn. This is the heritage of the servants of the Lord, and their righteousness is of me, saith the Lord"* (KJV). This is a powerful verse that many Christians claim and hold on to with all their might. But if these same Christians are rationalizing, justifying and protecting (perhaps even denying) wrong behaviors, wrong beliefs, wrong ideas, unforgiveness, bitterness, anger, and judgmentalness towards others, they are not going to be automatically protected against tongues of judgment rising up against them. A judgmental Christian cannot have it both ways.

Some believers, particularly those in certain charismatic circles, believe that claiming and speaking forth the Word of God will overcome any negative thing in their paths, regardless of who put it there. This is often bolstered by a self-inflicted "blindness" to any personal accountability in the hindering circumstance. (This particular line of thinking flourishes just like a mushroom, which grows best when hidden in the dark and fed decomposed waste.) Consequently, this Christian believes <u>all</u> seemingly negative things are from Satan, because God only does the good things. Right? Therefore, we can all claim full exemption from anything our unsurrendered souls might be contributing. It's all the devil's fault, isn't it? Wrong!

Satan loves this line of thinking, knowing it prevents us from determining the real source of our problems. Ezekiel 28 speaks of the guardian cherub (Lucifer) who was created beautiful, perfect, and with great wisdom. Granted, he did make a really bad judgment call when he challenged God, but Satan did not lose his superior intelligence when he was thrown out of heaven. He is still far smarter than any of us in ourselves.

When an unsurrendered soul repeatedly rejects the Holy Spirit's merciful entreaties to submit to His help, God will strive with that person in various ways. Sometimes surrender only seems to come through great crisis and loss. The Lord spoke recently to me about the "firewalls" in many lives, and I queried a building contractor about this term. The spiritual parallel was sobering, indeed. Firewalls are truly industrial strength in their ability to withstand fire, and there is usually great devastation from the flames and intense heat on every side of a firewall before it finally falls. When God cannot get a believer to pull down his or her own "industrial strength" strongholds to come into spiritual freedom, how much external fire and heat must He allow to come into a life before these "firewalls" will fall?

And the Beat Goes On

The key to deliverance from wrong behaviors of any kind is to expose the unmet needs driving them—

our bondage to them being only as strong as our attempts to hide them. The shame we feel over these needs is not condemnation from God. He knows the incredible force of the inward sources of our wrong feelings, the despair that overtakes us, the fears that haunt us, the anger that hurts us and others around us, the drives that push us to step over the line. He has given truth all through the Word about how we can let Him heal that which we can <u>never</u> fix ourselves.

Where does this ongoing pain from your past exist? In your memory. Coming out of wrong agreement with your bad memories terminates your soul's artificial "life support systems" for them. What happened to you years ago has no real life today, not unless you choose to let your soul infuse artificial life into the memory of it. Once you choose to expose the source of your pain's "life," the Holy Spirit can move in to spiritually neutralize your memories with His grace. After God's touch, the "bad" memories are no more threatening than a line in a phone book. They exist, but they have no power over you.

Symptoms Versus Sources

Many times our prayers seem to go unanswered because we pray for the wrong things. We pray about symptoms instead of shattering the strongholds protecting the actual source of the problem. That's like ministering to the runny nose of a person who is dying of double pneumonia. Focusing on symptoms keeps you from focusing on dismantling the strongholds to expose the sources. Satan knows full well that the strongholds in your life are his only edge over you. He's been accessing and attacking your whole being through them for years, trying to destroy you before you figured him out. By not dealing with your strongholds, you have actually been cooperating with Satan's plans for you and for those you pray for.

I prayed for twenty years that an alcoholic friend would lose his taste for alcohol after decades of drinking. Nothing happened. Then I began to pray binding and loosing prayers for him, and within a few weeks, this man declared that alcohol didn't taste good anymore. At the same time, I was teaching *Shattering Your Strongholds* to a group of inner-city Christians whose <u>former</u> lifestyles read like a Saturday-night police blotter—addicts, alcoholics, prostitutes, drug pushers, convicts, and at least one paroled murderer. I was very excited to tell them about this man losing his taste for alcohol.

One former addict/alcoholic shot down my reasoning for this deliverance as a bunch of "garbage." He said anyone who drank heavily for fifty years would never stop drinking just because it didn't taste good anymore. The person would continue to drink out of sheer habit. I then realized that for twenty years I had prayed against a symptom—the taste for alcohol. Nothing "happened" until I began binding this man's will to God's will and loosing the strongholds protecting the <u>source</u> or reason that he drank—then God delivered him. The strongholds protecting the source of his behavior had to be torn down before God's removal of his taste for alcohol would benefit him.

Even the strongest of faith-filled Christians repeatedly pray about symptoms. Perhaps months, even years, of sincere prayer have gone by in asking God to remove the <u>desire for</u> or <u>behavioral symptoms of</u> drugs in a child's life, or to take away an unfaithful mate's <u>desire for</u> other relationships. These prayers are not prayed in vain, but there is a reason for the long periods of no apparent answers. What good is accomplished if God removes an existing desire for drugs or adultery when the **sources fueling these behaviors still exist**? Sources not dealt with will continue to drive people to seek ways to take the edge off their pain and need.

Some people accept this as fact, prepare themselves to begin to use God's weapons and keys to stop the cycle, and then get tangled up in semantics of naming symptoms and sources. Don't go there! You do not have to name the symptoms or identify specific sources in your binding and loosing prayers. God is more than willing to take care of all of these details. Sometimes our prayers for our loved ones remain unanswered because we think we have "determined" the wrong sources and consequently pray amiss.

Learning to Pray Right Prayers

I rarely get sick, but last winter I began to feel the symptoms of a wicked flu that was going around. I promptly asked God to reveal the <u>source of these symptoms</u>, whether it was a natural viral infection or a door of access for a spiritual attack. In case it was a spiritual attack, I prayed and loosed all strongholds and wrong agreements from myself to close any doors I might have opened. In case it was a natural viral attack, I prayed for God to show me the source of any physical weakness that allowed the virus a place within me.

I believe He showed me the source of a <u>soulish weakness</u> on my part that had opened a door for both spiritual and physical attack. My soul had been quite unhappy for several weeks about some unkind words another person had said about me, and I had let my mind and emotions fuss over these words for days. I repented, released the offense, and loosed all of my soulish reactions until I felt any external access was closed. An open door in your soul can provide access to a natural and/or a demonic attack on your body. Any time a Christian's tripartite makeup of body, soul, and spirit are out of God's desired synergistic alignment, the soul and body are vulnerable.

Other peoples' actions towards us, i.e., speaking wrong words about us, can be orchestrated by Satan's pressuring of the strongholds in their souls. Our reactions to their behaviors can then cause wrong patterns of thinking in us which we may justify and rationalize instead of rejecting—a case of strongholds spawning strongholds. Such satanic manipulation of those around us always involves the devil throwing out a net, hoping to catch hold of open doors of access into our souls, too.

As the Holy Spirit reminded me of my soul's discontent and offense, I searched my soul to comply with closing its "doors" and rooting out of any of the resulting junky residue. In two days, I was free of the infection which was reported as hanging on in some people's bodies for weeks. Proverbs 26:2 (NIV) says, *"Like a fluttering sparrow or a darting swallow, an undeserved curse does not come to rest."* A curse that is not deserved cannot find a landing place unless you give it one. Being bound to God's will and loosing personally constructed, inner strongholds cuts off landing strips for curses. Obedience and submission to God's Word remove any remaining landing spots.

Word Curses

The primary sources of wrong behaviors are unmet needs, unhealed hurts, and unresolved issues. A secondary source of wrong behaviors is the effects and influences of human word curses. Occultic, demonic word curses can be cast upon Christians when there are open doors in their unsurrendered souls. But "natural" (as opposed to supernatural) word curses that bring about wrong behaviors happen far more frequently—wrong words spoken to you, about you, and by you. Such word curses have no expiration dates when they are left unchallenged. Some are spoken in the early years of our lives, some during the upheaval and turmoil of adolescence. Some are spoken in the present by parents, siblings, mates, bosses, acquaintances, etc. The issue is not when they are spoken or by whom. The real issue is that you don't have to live under the fallout from them. These word curses sound like this:

- "Give you a 50/50 chance of doing something right or wrong, you'll do it wrong every time."
- "I was always worried that you wouldn't succeed in life."
- "You'll probably end up just as crazy as your—."
- "Your Irish blood/Italian blood/Indian blood/African blood/etc., always makes you do—."

If your soul believes and comes into agreement with negative word curses as being truth, you will see everything in your life through the negative filter of those words. Such words already spoken cannot be erased, but you can loose their influence and effects from your life.

Remember that "loose" means smash, crush, shatter, break apart, destroy, melt, etc. It doesn't matter if you know or don't know the specific negative words that have been said, the prayer principle of binding and loosing will still work in nullifying their lingering effects in your life.

Pray like this example:

"Lord, I loose the influence and the effects of all word curses (known or unknown) spoken about me, to me, and by me. Forgive me for word curses I have spoken upon myself. I bind myself to the truth of the Word which tells me I can do all things through Jesus Christ, who strengthens me. I bind myself to the truth of the Word that Jesus has given me His peace which the world cannot take away. I bind myself to the truth of the Word that all things work together for my good. I am not limited by anyone else's opinions of my life and my abilities unless I choose to come into wrong agreement with such limitations. I loose every wrong agreement I've ever believed and entered into regarding negative words spoken to me or about me. I bind myself to the truth of the Word that I am a new creature in Christ. Old things have passed away. All things are new and waiting for me to receive them. In Jesus' name, Amen.

Healing

The same principle of deconstructing the power of word curses impacting your beliefs, attitudes, behaviors, etc., also extends to your health. Everyone has had some form of negative words spoken to them regarding health issues: "Men your age have a pretty high rate of prostate cancer, don't they?" "Your mother had all kinds of problems during the change of life, just like her mother and her grandmother. You probably will, too."

I believe in doctors, but people are being diagnosed today as having chemical imbalances, hormonal imbalances, hereditary weaknesses, predispositions to this or that, as well as hundreds of other things. While some may have all of the natural symptoms of these diagnosed conditions, when I pray for healing, I always loose the effects of word curses and wrong diagnoses spoken over the people I'm praying for. If their doctors didn't make wrong diagnoses or weren't speaking erroneously, nothing has been hurt. And something might be helped!

Sickness and disease certainly <u>can originate</u> from physical causes in our bodies. But sickness and disease <u>can remain</u> in our bodies because of wrong mind-sets that prevent us from receiving God's healing. Your body will do its best to come into alignment with whatever is most in control of your belief systems—medical diagnoses, generational infirmities, conventional wisdom, wrong mind-sets, word curses, wrong agreements, etc.

An interesting side issue here is that your soul will actually use old word curses and wrong beliefs about your health as an escape mechanism to avoid dealing with something it fears it cannot handle. This is a learned pattern of behavior that may become habitual because it seemed to worked so well the first time. If you frequently get "sick" whenever stress and pressure intensifies in your life, realize that you may be viewing your circumstances completely backwards. Your unsurrendered soul may be "sickening" your body so you are no longer accountable or even "able" to deal with what you feel inadequate to resolve.

Is There A Sign On the Back Bumper of My Car?

After my fifth rear-end auto accident which occurred a few years ago (each one happening while I was sitting at a stop light), I was told by a specialist, a physical therapist, and a chiropractor that I would never be the same again. This well-meaning "trio of cheer" said I would probably never regain the health and mobility I had formerly enjoyed, for I had sustained just too much trauma to my neck and back. As I was feeling poorly when these educated prognoses were given to me, I did not stand against the negative words being spoken and reinforced by all three voices.

I canceled some out-of-state ministry trips, shut down my activity schedule, and retreated into a shell. I emerged only to occasionally go to church and fulfill the most basic responsibilities of life. After about two months of this, I remember one day getting up out of my recliner, ever so slowly so nothing would hurt. As I lifted my foot to take a little step away from the chair, I heard the Lord speak loudly, *"GET ON WITH YOUR LIFE!"*

I raised my drooping head, straightened my spine, put my shoulders back, took a big step forward, and replied, "Yes, Sir!" I stepped out of the limitations of others' beliefs and understanding of conventional wisdom into God's unlimited reality. I immediately sensed the difference between having been in a mode of anticipating pain because the doctors said it would be there and being in a mode of expecting no pain because God seemed to be saying it wouldn't be there. I have never forgotten the tremendous new awareness I had at that moment of my choice to surrender to or refuse the pain. I saw clearly how I had been succumbing to familiar pain cycles whenever I experienced any tweak or twinge that indicated that a muscle spasm or headache was probably about to occur.

Reality, Hope, or Denial?

Some have misunderstood this testimony, believing that I am advocating denial of painful injuries. I'm not. I spent two painful months healing from the injuries I sustained in my last(!) auto accident. Obviously, that was long enough in God's eyes. I could have easily spent another several months in that same state if I hadn't chosen to respond to the voice of the Lord and step out of what had become familiar in order to walk into the rest of my life. I had been loosing wrong beliefs and self-limiting ideas from myself for several years, so I was aware of the potential of God's feelings about His plan for my life! (See Jer. 29:11.) This gave me a reason to want to get well. Some people who seem unable to get over sickness or injuries may have dozens of self-limiting wrong beliefs and ideas locked in place in their unsurrendered souls. If they have no hope for the unlimited potential of God's plan for them, they have little reason to hope to get well, either.

I think my three doctors probably made "medically correct" projections for my physical state. The factor they were unaware of was that I was continuing to pray the binding and loosing prayers (if somewhat feebly), even while I was in the worst pain. When prayed in faith, these prayers are always working, whether visible manifestations are showing or not. I appreciated these medical experts' caring treatment, but I was not bound to their future projections. Neither was God!

Always remember that your body is a follower, and it will trot right along behind whatever or whoever seems to be in control of your belief systems. Your body has a strong natural need to be in agreement with the rest of your tripartite being. I believe this need is so strong that the body will alter its own chemical makeup, even to its own detriment, in order to come into alignment with any intellectually and emotionally powerful wrong agreements existing in your soul. Such an agreement could be fear of cancer when none exists. Medical science has proven that a persistent fear of getting a certain disease can eventually produce the symptoms of that disease. Those symptoms can produce devastating physical effects in the body, even in effect becoming the actual disease.

But the other side of that same incredible ability of your body to redefine its own chemistry is greatly encouraging! When it recognizes your regenerated, renewed spirit-man as being in complete control of your belief systems, it will alter its natural chemistry to come into agreement with this belief system. Glory to God! This is not denial, this is divine direction, Christian!

Now, consider whether or not you have entered into agreement with and thereby accepted ungodly generational beliefs about heredity-controlled physical weaknesses in your family. Have you come into wrong agreement with intellectual beliefs, conventional wisdom, and/or medical beliefs regarding your health? In the face of symptoms that won't go away, test results that aren't good, and bad news from the doctors, are you in agreement with God's Word that says He is still in control? If He's in control and you're bound to His will, you will be in the palm of His hand—whatever happens.

Is your regenerated spirit or your unsurrendered soul in charge of your belief system? Your life may depend on knowing. The following prayer is a collection of ways of praying for healing.

Training-Wheel Prayer
for Receiving Healing

Lord, I have needs in my physical body, the temple you chose and fashioned for me to dwell in—the same temple you have chosen to dwell in by your Holy Spirit. If I have pursued false gods and allowed my soul to practice idolatry, forgive me, cleanse me of the effects of this wicked way, and empower me to purge my soul and my physical temple of these wrong desires. I know that wrong pursuit and use of food, money, alcohol, drugs, sex, and power can all be the pursuit of false gods.

Lord, I know I cannot run after my soul's wrong desires and expect you to continue to heal the effects of my ongoing disobedience. I ask you to confront my soul with any area I am denying, even as I am loosing denial from myself and seeking your truth. I want to be in good health to pursue you and the Kingdom work you have ordained for me to do. I bind the inward parts of my being—my mind, will, and emotions—to your truth at any cost to my soul. I loose any resistance my soul has to any area of your Word. Holy Spirit, be the watchman on the wall if I stumble or turn aside from walking in the will of the Father. Sound a warning in whatever way is necessary to quickly reveal my error.

I loose any layers I have laid down within my soul to protect any natural weaknesses, deceptions, or half-

truths that have negatively impacted my belief system. Let your mercy and grace fill me, Father, as I strip away the grave clothes from my soul and my flesh. I don't seek just a deliverance from the symptoms of physical infirmity, Lord—I want to know the source of such a conflict within me. Show me if my symptoms are a result of soulish indulgence, an acceptance of and agreement with error, a spiritual attack, or an invasion into my body by an infectious organism. If these symptoms have been caused by a spiritual attack, Father, I loose every one of the enemy's hindrances and devices from my life. If these symptoms have been caused by a deception of my soul, I loose the strongholds, grave clothes, and lies that have introduced this confusion into my physical body. I loose word curses, generational bondages, and wrong teachings from myself.

If this sickness has been caused by an infectious organism, show me the weakness in my immune system that has allowed it to find entrance into my body. Show me if I am eating wrong. Show me or if I am relying on medications and man-made answers that are not in your will for me. Show me the source of the entrance this thing found in me. I loose, strip, and destroy the power and hold of this infection or disease from my body. I loose, strip, and destroy the reproductive cycle of this organism. I loose any wrong beliefs, any wrong attitudes, any bitterness from my soul that are sustaining vulnerability and weakness in my body. I ask you to reveal any other sources of access that are in me. In Jesus' name, Amen.

"Generational-Bondage" Thinking

Another secondary source of wrong behaviors is generational-bondage thinking. I believe generational bondages are directly linked to our souls' agreement with and acceptance of generational-bondage patterns of thinking. Some generational-bondage thinking can be induced by transference of spirits, but I believe most passing on of such thought patterns come through a much simpler, ordinary format.

I find it interesting that Webster (in part) describes the word hereditary, which I always believed to be just physical traits, as also meaning the attitudes and beliefs transmitted from one generation to another. Many family characteristics repeated from one generation to another have little to do with evil spirits, chromosomes, or gene pools. They are more likely to be the result of the daily exposure of one unsurrendered soul to another. If there are strong areas of anger, unforgiveness, impatience, and/ or mistrust in an unsurrendered soul, its verbal expressions to others will be saturated with anger, unforgiveness, impatience, and/or mistrust. Whenever people are repeatedly put together in close quarters, there will be a communal sharing of negative characteristics and prejudices. If we would all begin loosing negative beliefs about ourselves and one another, think of the familial, racial, and cultural conflicts we might overcome.

Lord, I loose the influence and the effects of all generational bondages (actual or perceived, known or unknown) that may be limiting my spiritual life and liberty in Christ Jesus. Forgive me for accepting these self-fulfilling generational deceptions as being truth. I bind myself to the truth of the Word which tells me I am a new creature in Christ. I bind myself to the truth of the Word that I am now a part of the family of God, with a new parentage and bloodline. I bind myself to the truth of the Word that He is the vine and I am a branch of that vine, drawing all good sustenance from Him. I cannot be limited by anyone else's opinions of my life and my abilities unless I choose to come into wrong agreement with such limitations. All things are new and waiting for me to receive them. In Jesus' name, Amen.

Christian Families in Bondage

Actual spiritual generational bondage does occur, and it can even be passed from a non-believing generation to a Christian generation if no one identifies and breaks the cycle. Suppose two brand-new Christians meet and enter into a relationship. They experience strong feelings of lust for each other, resulting from the spiritually-unresolved, prior sexual promiscuity in both of their lives. Upon deciding to marry, they commit to abstinence from any premarital sex because of their genuine love for the Lord and His commandments. Unsure of how to ask Him to help them with their increasingly strong sexual desires, they fight to overcome their lustful feelings through sheer willpower. They have no understanding that their vulnerability to lust is coming out of their unmet needs, and because of their strongholds creating doors of access, evil spirits are compounding their problems.

The two Christians marry, and they are both very relieved that they have now "legitimized" their lustful feelings for each other through their marriage vows. But, a marriage ceremony in a big church does not automatically close the doors on wrong spirits that have known access to individuals' souls. Nor will a Christian marriage ceremony automatically turn lust into godly sexual desire. The doors of access to spirits which were previously opened by this couple's prior acts of fornication would only be closed through:

> 1) Repentance (confession of and determination to turn from) by each one for past sins, and believing by each one in God's resulting impartation of divine forgiveness for and cleansing of them.
> 2) Prayer, both individually and together, binding themselves to God's will and the truth of His Word, also the binding of their minds to the mind of Christ to receive peace.
> 3) Dismantling their souls' areas of control through prayer by loosing their strongholds, wrong agreements, and wrong desires to expose their deepest unmet needs. Asking for His grace and mercy to flow into and heal every needy, hurting, and confused area in their souls.
> 4) Loosing any and all soul-ties formed through the previous acts of fornication. (Look for more about soul-ties in Chapter 7).

Not understanding this, this hypothetical couple conceive a child who is brought into a home where wrong spirits have access. When that small child shows an abnormal interest in sexual things beyond his years, everyone seem confused about why. Did someone molest the child, was it the fault of today's ungodly media, did it come from an experience with unsaved children? What could cause the precious little child of this lovely young Christian couple to behave like this? The parents, and their spiritual and psychological counselors, seek the cause of the aberrant behavior outside of the home.

All the time, heartbreakingly, a spiritual generational bondage was passed down to the child from the parents who were unwittingly giving access to wrong spirits. The baby could have been shielded by one knowledgeable parent, but both parents were ignorant of their open doors of access. The parents weren't in sin as they consummated their marriage in the eyes of God. But because of never having been taught about their souls' disorder and misalignment, about the power of their strongholds to create open doors of access to wrong spirits, they were unable to protect the purity of the spiritual inheritance their child should have automatically derived from being born into a Christian home.

Training-Wheel Prayer
to Break Wrong Behaviors

Lord, I desire to be free from the wrong behaviors hindering my life, my health, my witness, and my work for you. These behaviors are sin, but they are not the source of the problem in me—they are but the symptoms. I'm tired of trying to overcome these symptoms, trying to get victory over them, trying to understand and deal with them only to have them return again and again. I want to sever the root and expose the source of these behaviors to you, clear down to the hair roots.

Jesus, so many things have happened in my life that I have believed were responsible for my shortcomings. I loose that lie right now. I have been responsible for some things, but I was not responsible for all of them. These are the ones that I have the most trouble with, Jesus, the traumatic things I had no choice in at the time. But, right now, I am going to exercise my choice to be set free from any and all influences from past experiences in my life. Empower me to receive the fullness of your grace and love to uncover the layers of self-protection that I've laid down over all of these unresolved issues. I don't want to hold on to the pain, confusion, doubt, anger, bitterness, unforgiveness, and hatred that just keeps boiling up out of them. I want them all gone.

I don't want to manifest these wrong behaviors in my life anymore. Lord, I confess that many of the behaviors have been my own self-centered attempts to pacify and take the edge off my deeper hurts and needs. But it's not working! Forgive me for ever listening to my unsurrendered, proud, stubborn soulish nature, and believing that I could find something or someone who would fix me.

I loose every wall, every stronghold, every word curse that I or anyone else has ever spoken over my life. I loose every layer and attempt of my soul to protect, hide, or fulfill my needs. I know now that no one can ever fix me at my deepest level of pain and need except you. As I strip away the efforts of my own will to keep you out of the places where even I am afraid to go, please make me whole in you.

Teach me, Holy Spirit, to recognize the agendas of my soul, to identify soulish attempts to bury the sources of my anger and resentment. Teach me to recognize my own self-attempts to manipulate others to ensure my own personal damage control. I choose to turn to you for strength, for mercy, for healing, and for deliverance from the dregs and residue of my old ways. I choose to reach out for the peace that only Jesus can give to me, for it is the only way to overcome the confusion and torment that I have tried to drown with alcohol, food, drugs, and wrong relationships. I choose to now face the fact that my own attempts to anesthetize and block out the pain and confusion have only kept you out. I need you in my deepest inner parts, Lord.

I need your healing love—I choose your guidance and direction—and I loose all wrong beliefs and attitudes I've ever learned from the world that would turn me from seeking only you. I commit all that I am and all that I am not to you, Lord. In Jesus' name, Amen.

5

Unmet Needs, Unhealed Hurts, Unresolved Issues

All of us have needs we have given up expecting any fulfillment of, hurts that still ache years after they were inflicted, and troubling issues we've never been able to understand. We've learned to bury the needs, pacify the pain, stuff the issues, cope with the lack, deny the hopelessness, and fear the sense of helpless vulnerability this creates in us. We do this because it is expected of us, while we live out lives that are not what we had hoped they might someday be.

Our lives today often seem to be consumed by pressures, responsibilities, deadlines, and the expectations of others. We generally do our best to respond appropriately, but we end up reacting to this heavy load—feeling angry, put upon, and abused. This makes us feel guilty and more resentful. So, we have to build more strongholds to justify still more wrong feelings we have no idea how to process and clear from our souls. As

Charlie Brown would say in the "Peanuts" comic strip, whenever life closes in on him, "Arghhhhhhhhhhh!"

The perfect-case scenario would have been that we all grew up with as much love and nurturing as we could hold; we were never physically, mentally, or emotionally abused; we were never the target of negative words; and we were never neglected, rejected, or betrayed. But because imperfect people were usually involved in the life-process of our formative years, most of us ended up imperfect as well. Still, such a perfect-case scenario is not forever lost to us. When we surrender fully to Him, God has all the love and nurturing we can hold; He will never physically, mentally, or emotionally abuse us; He will never speak word curses over us; and He will never neglect, reject, or betray us. Our unsurrendered souls are the only factor preventing such an impartation of His love right now.

Your Soul's First Line of Defense

Your unsurrendered soul's first line of defense against any interference with its position of power is to build strongholds out of your mind's human logic, reasoning, arguments, justification, denial, and defensiveness, which guard the wrong ideas, beliefs, attitudes, motives, and patterns of thinking that are holding you in bondage. If your soul can keep you trapped by these strongholds, you will never dig deeper to dismantle the bottom-line defense of its control structure.

Your mind is the battlefield where your unsurrendered soul and Satan wage their war for the control of your destiny. This is the part of you that strongly needs renewal after the salvation of your spirit.

Romans 12:2 (AMP) tells us, "*Do not be conformed to this world—this age, fashioned after and adapted to its external, superficial customs. But be transformed (changed) by the [entire] renewal of your mind—by its new ideals and its new attitude—so that you may prove [for yourselves] what is the good and acceptable and perfect will of God, even the thing which is good and acceptable and perfect [in His sight for you].*" The strongholds in your mind must be shattered before its complete transformation and renewal can ever be accomplished. When these strongholds have been deconstructed, the rest of the workings of the unsurrendered soul become visible.

Facts Cannot Be Loosed

Much childhood trauma is sustained from factual events that did happen and cannot be changed. I wish we could loose the facts of neglect, abuse, and lack of love from lives—our own as well as others. But when neglect, abuse, and a lack of love really existed, these are facts. Facts cannot be loosed. Because of these errors and omissions in your early life, three things happened: unmet needs, unhealed hurts, and unresolved issues were birthed. These areas of vulnerability produce the pain, fear, and doubt that keep you from fully surrendering to an intimate relationship with God. They are the source of the fear and pain that your soul unleashes whenever you move too close to God—the neediness, hopelessness, insecurity, anger, confusion, and wrong desires that keep bringing defeat into your life.

Have you ever wondered how a powerful message from the Word of God on Sunday sometimes barely lasts through Monday night? Or how a special gift, a new car, or a new friend causes you to think "this" will surely change your life—but by morning your joy is already leaking away? I knew one Christian who repeatedly seemed to get lower than low. Many Christians gave him scriptural promises, encouragement, and loving acceptance, praying with him until he was uplifted. Within two days, he would be lower than low again. Several of us went through this pattern with him over and over until finally I said in exasperation, "Mark, you leak!" Thinking I was just frustrated, I had no idea this was a prophetic truth.

The unmet needs, unhealed hurts, and unresolved issues in your unsurrendered soul are like bottomless holes. Regardless of how much good preaching, singing, praise and worship, prayer, love, and attention comes into your life and uplifts you, they immediately begin to leak back out of the holes in your soul. No amount of money, alcohol, drugs, sex, material things, relationships, or food can ever fill up those gaping holes! Only God can, but don't get upset at Him for not yet doing so. Right above the soul's three "holey" sources of need, pain, and confusion—the unmet needs, unhealed hurts, and unresolved issues—lies the soul's bottom-line defense against being dethroned. God will not violate that self-erected defense system. I believe there are two ways this power structure can be deconstructed, one bad and one good.

The bad way is when the soul becomes overwhelmed by the sustained intensity of the drives pushing up out of the three sources. The mind, will, and emotions simply can't take the overload anymore of being driven to fix that which is unfixable. Having no backup support system, the soul simply begins to come apart under the pressure. The corrosive acidity of the unmet needs, unhealed hurts, and unresolved issues have eaten away too much of its infrastructure and the holes have become too big. I picture them becoming like whirlpools, slowly sucking everything down into darkness. When the soul collapses in upon itself, minds snap, emotions break, and the will to live is gone. Praise God, He can reverse this, and will, when others stop to pray!

The good way the power structure of the unsurrendered soul can be deconstructed is through a cooperative work between the believer and God. The believer looses the layers, walls, strongholds, and all "high things" that have stood between himself and God. Into this now unblocked soul, God pours grace, mercy, and healing. The soul, with its walls and strongholds down, receives and is made whole. <u>Understanding this cooperative work is the purpose of this book.</u>

Our Part

Because of the fallen Adamic sin nature we are naturally born with, we come into this world with a strong attraction for darkness. Once Jesus Christ comes to live within us through our new spiritual birth, Colossians 1:13 (NIV) says God rescues us from the dominion of darkness. At that point, the only control Satan can effect over us personally is by trying to access our unsurrendered souls. God has probably delivered us from the power of the enemy hundreds of times that we are not even aware of, but He will not deliver us from the power of our own souls! We must choose to stop them from creating open doors of access to the devil.

To do this, we must take apart the power infrastructure of our unsurrendered souls. This is basically the meaning of Paul's command that we are to crucify our own flesh, our unsurrendered soulish nature. It is much easier to resist and reject the pull of our old natures when we are constantly pressuring our souls' defense systems. This happens as we keep loosing and rejecting old thoughts patterns, old memory tapes, wrong beliefs, and wrong attitudes, while binding our minds, wills, and emotions to God's greater purposes.

Then we begin loosing the "grave clothes" that our unsurrendered souls insist upon dragging around. None of us can loose the facts of our past experiences, but we can loose the deception, pain, fear, and anxiety we've learned to associate with our memories of them. Traumatic memories do not need to be twelve-stepped, denied, or coped with—they need to be spiritually neutralized! And the Holy Spirit is truly the Great Neutralizer! This work of healing grace in your life can't flow into your pain if you don't know how to make your soul release its "safeguards" protecting your hurt.

When you do not understand God's grace, you believe you must constantly reinforce your own self-protective defenses. This puts you under constant pressure to patrol the walls around your areas of vulnerabilty, always on guard against someone or something finding a way to get to your unhealed hurts. That is both exhausting and counter-productive to becoming a joyful, victorious Christian overcomer. You have to stop trusting in your own self-defense mechanisms to take on God's divine defenses.

Before continuing on, here is a descriptive review

of the three souces of the pain, need, and confusion in our unsurrendered souls:

Unmet needs are birthed when something good that should have happened didn't.

Unhealed hurts are birthed when something bad that should not have happened did.

Unresolved issues are birthed when you are incapable of processing such occurrences in a positive spiritual, mental, emotional, and physical manner.

Unmet Needs

An unmet need is like a ravenous wild animal. You can try to avoid it, kill it, or appease it. We often try to avoid, kill, or appease our unmet needs. God just wants to meet them. We don't think too often about making a way for Him to get in close enough to do it.

Instead, we think if we just had the right man or woman in our lives, or the right job, education, hair, weight, house, car, or clothes, then things would be better. When we've clung so desperately to the fantasy of attaining one of these carrots that the world has dangled in front of us for so long, it is very scary to admit that not one of them can meet our needs. It can seem even scarier to tear down the protective strongholds, throw out all those wrong ideas, and stand stripped and emotionally naked before God, admitting, "I guess there isn't anything this world has that will ever meet my needs. Now what do I do?"

We have all tried so many things—buying off, burying, denying our unmet needs. The problem is that our unmet needs, like wild tigers, reject any efforts to pacify them but momentarily, and they come driving right back after us again and again. We can try to kill them, and some have succeeded by their own suicides. Or, we can try to appease them with offerings of more relationships, sex, alcohol, food, drugs, etc. These coping behaviors only "quiet" the needs temporarily. They lay down for a while and are not as prone to push for satisfaction, until the "fix" wears off. Then they begin to prowl again.

We have all cried out over and over for God to fix the pain, fix the neediness, fix our mate, or send someone who will make us feel good about ourselves. God is more than willing to help if you will give Him <u>any sort of access to the unmet need</u>. But your soul has built its strongholds to keep Him out. That is why He has said, *"Tear down your strongholds."*

Unmet Needs Produce Wrong Desires

Wrong desires generally come from an inner drive to satisfy an unmet need that has been in your life for a long time. Behavior driven by unmet needs is often perceived as a weakness of character or a personal failing. For example, someone who has a deep, unmet need for love will constantly get into wrong relationships. Someone who has a deep, unmet need for security may be a compulsive shopper and hoarder. Someone who has a deep, unmet need for acceptance may fish for compliments all the time. Someone who has a deep, unmet need to feel necessary may constantly compete for positions of authority he cannot effectively handle.

Such "acting out" of unmet needs is rarely considered socially acceptable, particularly among those who are worried about their own unmet needs. There are usually consequences from our attempts to meet our own neediness, such as being rejected, ridiculed, ostracized, and criticised. This causes any needy person to ultimately see his or her unmet needs as personal weaknesses rather than needs the Lord wants to meet. Strongholds are erected around the needs in the hope of hiding them from others. "Out of sight," perhaps, but the needs still exist. And they are still exerting internal pressure which still manifests itself in wrong desires, wrong behaviors, and wrong reactions.

Wrong desires that come out of these unmet needs have the potential to escalate into powerfully destructive drives to achieve their fulfillment. Wrong desires bring about the destruction of marriages and wrong desires bring about wrong marriages. Oh, how often I pray with lonely, needy people, pleading with them to turn to God for healing before they search for someone they hope will meet their unmet needs. I ask them to pray the following training-wheel prayer:

Training-Wheel Prayer
to Prepare for a Mate

I bind myself to your will and purposes for my future, Lord, so your plans will be fulfilled in my life—whether they are plans I think I want or not. You know the tug on my heart when I see a loving husband and wife. I long for such a relationship, but if I desire a mate only to fill an empty place in my heart instead of seeking to fill it with you, show me how to change.

I bind myself to pure motives for wanting a mate, not just to meet my unmet needs, to heal my unhealed hurts, or to resolve my unresolved issues. That is placing unrealistic expectations on any human. No man or woman could ever fulfill such expectations. you alone can do that. You alone can fill me with grace, bathe me in love, meet my needs, heal my hurts, and resolve my questions and issues.

I loose the layers of self-protection and self-defense I have laid down over these areas of vulnerability in my life. Jesus, I want to let you get to these sources of my neediness and loneliness and pain so you can heal them with your supernatural power, grace, mercy, and love. I've felt like I've been trapped in a vacuum where nothing is ever enough. I don't want to be needy and hurting any longer. I want to be a fully satisfied source of hope and blessing to others. No one will get hope from watching a life that is always unsatisfied, needy, and in pain. But I know that many can receive hope from a life that <u>was once like that</u>, but has now been changed and made whole by you!

I do not want to force my way past your will into a relationship only to see my needs suck all of the joy, peace, and life out of a mate. Lord, forgive me for the times I have blamed you for my loneliness, for my lack of having someone to care for me. I know that you have been protecting me and others from the hurt and heartbreak a wrong relationship brings. I loose all of the discouragement, deception, and denial in my soul that has kept you from getting into its deepest parts—the places so dark and lonely that even I won't go there. Lord, I will let you fix me in whatever way you need to fix me.

Jesus, if there is a special man/woman you have chosen and are preparing just for me, I bind him/her to your will and purposes. I ask that you draw him/her into a strong, whole relationship with you, Jesus. I ask that you teach him/her to see you as the focus and very center of his/her life, just as I am asking you to do with me. I bind myself and him/her to your timing. I will not seek to find any such person through my own efforts. You will know if and when the time is right for both of us to come together into a relationship.

Lord, if you desire for me to remain wholly devoted to and single-minded towards you, then pour your grace and mercy into me and mark me as yours alone. Teach me how to come into a covenant of intimacy with you like I have never known before. Teach me to hear your voice and respond to every word of your love. Teach me how to love you, to bless you, and to minister to you. Teach me how to come apart from the world and go with you into that never-yet-entered secret meeting place that is just ours. Teach me how to receive whatever you want to give to me. In Jesus' name, Amen.

Johnny-Be-Good and Johnny-Be-Bad Syndrome

Wrong relationships are the results of attempts to meet one's own unmet needs. I once read an interesting comment in a newspaper that revealed an answer to a long-standing question I have had. Why do some people, particularly women, reject nice, safe relationships for wrong relationships? I've decided to call this the Johnny-Be-Good/Johnny-Be-Bad syndrome.

"Judy," who has deep, unmet needs in her life, never has felt special or precious to anyone. Johnny-Be-Good, a kind, good-hearted man, comes into Judy's life and treats her as someone very special. Even though this is what she has always believed would take away the grawing need in her innermost parts, she isn't interested. Why not? Because Johnny-Be-Good is nice to everyone. Therefore, when he is kind and good to her, she has no way of perceiving that she is special or different from everyone else. After all, Johnny-Be-Good treats her just like he treats everybody.

Johnny-Be-Bad roars into town, ready for trouble. He clearly doesn't like anybody, doesn't trust anybody, and doesn't treat anyone nice. But he is attracted to Judy. So he tells her she is the only person he has ever met who is this special. Bingo! Being the only person he cares for and "trusts," Judy now has tangible, emotional proof that she is special. Johnny-Be-Bad has said so, and now he becomes her mission in life. If she can meet his needs, love him enough to change him, she will finally prove she could accomplish what no one else ever could.

Unmet needs drive people into many unhealthy, co-dependent relationships. The following prayer is for those needing to recognize unhealthy relationships in their lives:

Training-Wheel Prayer
for Wrong-Relationships

Jesus, I'm so tired of running away from my fears that you won't be enough when everyone else has gone home, and I'm all alone. Your Word says you have longed to be everything to me. The Word says my eyes and my ears can never begin to comprehend the things you and the Father have planned for me. The Word says you and the Father have come and made your home in me. Lord, what is preventing me from accepting that as truth and reality at every level of my being? Why do I fear being alone, apart from human company? What are the unresolved issues in me that cause me to doubt your love and resist intimacy with you? I loose the lie of my soul that says you won't be enough.

Jesus, you have said that we are now so compatible that I am like a branch of your vine. I bind myself to the truth of my relationship with you—loosing my concept of it in order to receive your reality of it. I loose all of the half-truths, lies, denial, and self-centered beliefs that I have listened to. I want to make more room for you in my life by stripping away the clutter and baggage in my soul so that you can pour your revelation and insight into me. Then I can learn the secrets that abide only within a deep and intimate knowledge of you.

Lord, I will no longer seek relationships with men/ women in order to try to fill up the emptiness inside of me. That emptiness is for you and you alone to fill. I will not try to meet my own needs, and I loose every desire and motive that has driven me to do so in the past. I will not let my unmet needs drive me any longer. I will not hang on to wrong relationships in order to seek relief from my unhealed hurts.

You, Jesus, are the only one who can give understanding to me that I am special and unique in the eyes of the Father. You alone can resolve the confusion and the painfully uncomfortable issues of my life. No man or woman can do this. When I believe others can do this, I make myself vulnerable to their control and manipulation. When I believe a man or woman can meet all my needs, I make myself vulnerable to soul-ties and deception.

Lord, I ask you to mark my relationships. Show me if I'm in wrong agreement with other people hoping to get what I think I need. Show me who is using me to meet their needs. Show me those I am trying to use for any purpose. Lord, help me find the right relationships, the right close friends, the right alliances that are in alignment with your will for my destiny. Give me divine favor with those who are to become my prayer partners, my best friends, my ministry partners, even a mate. Let me be a vessel of truth and grace and love to them. Show me how to impart to others in purity of heart. In Jesus' name, Amen.

Sacrificial Offerings to Unmet Needs

Do you think "sacrificial offerings" to an "unknown god" never occur in true Christianity? Guess again. As the Body of Christ, many of us are focused on fellowshipping with food. We plan our fellowships around food, we hold potluck dinners and covered-dish suppers, we celebrate marriage with buffets and sit down dinners, we come together after funerals over food, we go out after church services for food. Alcohol, drugs, and wrong company can be avoided—but food is everywhere we turn! Consequently, food is the most common substance used by the Christian to pacify gnawing unmet needs. It is also the substance abuse most studiously avoided during public altar calls.

For some time now I've received letters from Christians who were struggling with their weight. These requests for help came from those who are moderately overweight as well as those who are extremely overweight. Weight is an issue I've struggled with myself—and still do—so I have a heart that quickly hears the need in the words of someone who feels guilt and a sense of failure for being overweight. For those who are expending unnecessary energy struggling with guilt over a failure to lose weight, rather than productively seeking His help, know this: When God measures us, He puts the tape around our hearts, not our hips! God is not judging our weight, He is wanting to heal the source of the drive we're ineffectively trying to appease.

The answer to good health, energy, and an active lifestyle is not found in dieting as usual, the answer is in learning how to let God get into the unmet needs. Sacrificial offerings to those needs are only a temporary, front-line defense measure with unpleasant consequences!

There are some good "programs" and Christian "support groups" for people with weight problems. But God's Word and His answers have never been dependent upon our being in the vicinity of a support group or having the money for expensive workbooks, tapes, and videos. I've been binding myself to God's will, loosing strongholds, stripping off layers over my unmet needs, unhealed hurts, and unresolved issues for several years now. I feel I've made some inroads into the areas of eating for wrong reasons. Yet I'm still aware of wanting to turn to "comfort food" when I'm tired, feeling needy, and feeling vulnerable.

We eat food our body doesn't need for many different reasons. Sometimes we eat just to chemically elevate our moods in a seemingly "Christian-approved" way. Eating chocolate always makes me feel "better" temporarily. That's the key word: temporarily. The later and still-future consequences can also be ignored, temporarily: sugar crashes (lows), headaches, weight gain, guilt. Sometimes we eat to dull our thoughts, sometimes to literally drug ourselves into oblivion. Sometimes we eat to compensate for feeling rejected, unloved, or inadequate. Some eat to try to "fill up" a sense of great emptiness inside themselves.

We may be conscious of some of these things in our lives, but there are other things our souls have buried beneath our level of consciousness. And our souls are not about to let these scary things be exposed without some stripping and loosing. The following prayer is for those who want to put food into its proper perspective in their lives:

Training-Wheel Prayer
for Food Addiction

Father, help me to understand this wondrous vessel you have fashioned for me to use and for your Spirit to dwell in—my body. Teach me to understand that you have endowed it with an innate knowing of what it does and doesn't need as well as when it needs it in order to function at its maximum performance. Help me recognize when <u>my unsurrendered soul is trying to use this wondrous vessel to help it blot out need and pain.</u> God, I now choose to issue this edict to every part of my being: **I will no longer be like a puppet responding to the pulling of whatever strings my unsurrendered soul might use to try to control me!**

Lord, help me to return to eating for sustenance and energy only. Help me to recognize hunger as the reason for eating and the cessation of hunger pangs for the reason to stop eating. I know I have overloaded and abused the systems of my body by requiring it to constantly digest food. I have allowed myself to become both the abuser and the abused. O God, forgive me and help me to return to your truth and your wisdom for my body.

I bind my body, soul, and spirit to your will, confessing that I know I have not been doing what's best for me to do. I loose from myself all wrong attitudes about food. I loose wrong emotional reactions that I have formerly used to validate eating comfort foods. I loose my soul's desire to stuff my body in order to dull my senses, when it is reacting to reactivated pain. I choose to separate the needs of the normal physical functions of my body from the unnatural neediness of my soul.

I bind the inward parts of my body to your will and purposes—my stomach, digestive system, heart, liver, colon, circulatory system, brain, nervous system, as well as everything else you've created within me, Father. I bind the inward parts of my soul's belief system to your will and truth, Father. I bind myself to your truth, and I loose wrong ideas I have accepted as "truth" from man's ideas about good and bad food.

I loose self-justification, self-desire, self-deception, and the self-denial that I have allowed my soul to layer over my unmet needs—keeping you out. Forgive me, Lord, for using food to try to take the edge off the drives of these needs, rather than letting you closer so you can meet them. Forgive me for using food to medicate and even drug myself when the pain of unhealed hurts seemed too much, too overwhelming. Help me to seek the food of freedom, healing, joy, and peace that fine-tunes and streamlines my life—the spiritual food in your Word. In Jesus' name, Amen.

Using Your Vulnerability Positively

I recently recognized a very important factor in my usual reactions to feeling vulnerable. This recognition immediately followed an emotional healing clinic where I ministered. Being stretched to bring fresh understanding and answers to expectant people there, I found myself receiving fresh understanding as well.

The morning after the clinic ended, I felt incredibly vulnerable, even weepy, in every fiber of my being. I was confused as to how I could feel this way after so many hours spent in delivering the Word and receiving back from the other ministers as well. All I could think was, "What is my problem? I should feel great right now." Old patterns of thinking would have resulted in my running through all of the religious "rituals" I usually turn to when I feel vulnerable: quoting power Scriptures to overlay my feelings of vulnerabilty; praying for strength to overlay my weakness of vulnerability; singing praise songs to overlay my fear of vulnerability; sacrificial offerings of comfort foods to "self-medicate" the symptoms of vulnerability.

We all have our religious rituals that we can call up and run just like computer programs. Most of the time, mine are successful in helping me to get past my moments of feeling defenseless and vulnerable. But this time, I recognized something I had never seen before. Vulnerability has a great potential for letting God move in where He's not been free to enter before. Rather than trying to overcome the vulnerability and be the mighty "woman of God" I sometimes picture myself to be, I saw it as a possible doorway to push closer to God.

I cried out this following prayer: *O God, my self-defense systems are completely down right now. Here I am with little between me and you. Please take advantage of this openness and pour your mercy and grace into any areas that are being exposed. I'm not sure what specifically caused them to open right now, therefore, I don't know how long they will remain exposed. But I ask you to pour everything into me that you can. I will not war against feelings of vulnerability anymore, I will use them to run straight into you. I now see my vulnerability as an open door of opportunity to know you more intimately. I'll use vulnerability to receive you at a deeper level than I've ever allowed before. In Jesus' name, Amen.*

Unhealed Hurts

Unhealed hurts come into being when something awful that shouldn't have happened, did. Acts of betrayal, rejection, and abuse all create unhealed hurts in children, adolescents, and adults. But we have been taught by the conventional wisdom of the world to place undue emphasis upon having had imperfect people in our lives "who should have known better" instead of having perfect people "who would have known better" and done what we needed them to do. When our unhealed hurts are telegraphing the pain loud and clear, it doesn't matter one jot or tittle to us that in the flawed world we live in, no human ever has been or is now capable of providing a perfect balance of support to us.

When we are in constant pain from unhealed hurts, we often don't even know how to receive whatever support or help is available to us right now. Those who have deep, unhealed hurts generally experience overwhelming feelings of doubt, pain, fear, distrust, and suspicion towards others. This creates hidden agendas in all of our relationships, for we believe we must also "guard" against further pain even while we are trying to reach out for help.

There is a term some physical therapists and chiropractors use called "guarding." This is when people resist someone's efforts to adjust that which is misaligned in their lives because they are afraid of the pain increasing. Most of us have painful areas that our souls are fiercely "guarding" against any more pain, and we've thrown up strongholds all around them. Remember that the threefold statement of purpose of the unsurrendered soul is, "No more pain, no more pain, no more pain."

The Holy Spirit is like a "holy chiropractor" who wants to readjust our misalignment with God, but our misaligned souls have to voluntarily cooperate with this intimate kind of ministry. True intimacy is always voluntary. Forced intimacy against any kind of "guarding" is a violation, and God will not violate His children. Many, many Christians desperately cling to their wrong beliefs and fears born out of painful experiences that have taught them to equate intimacy with violation, danger, and betrayal. Before they were ever able to choose voluntary intimacy, they were intimately violated by deception, betrayal, and/or force. Some Christians unconsciously use this fact to justify distancing themselves from intimacy with God.

Unhealed Hurts: Damaged Leaders

There is no educational/professional/spiritual training or self-discipline that will ever keep a spiritual leader's "buried" unforgiveness, confusion, anger, hurt, and/or neediness from ultimately leaking out into his (or her) ministry. Trying to "self-contain" these feelings is never effective, because hidden things in your soul are always a prime target of the devil. Satan can't read your mind, but he does keep excellent records on everything about you. He knows which painful "experiences" you've overcome and which ones you have tried to bury. If he can't get at your buried pain directly, then he'll get others around you to pressure the "hot spots" in your unhealed hurts.

This serious danger to your healing and spiritual growth does not stem from any of Satan's plans against you—the danger lies within your soul's continuing efforts to control the unhealed hurt. Satan will eventually maneuver someone into stepping on those hot spots of pain and you'll explode—just like a stepped-on, capped-up tube of toothpaste lying on hard tile floor!

In one meeting I was leading, a well-meaning person I'll call "Q" (in the early stages of his ministry) made a serious error because of an unhealed hurt in his own life. One struggling Christian, "J," was just beginning, through receiving personal ministry that night, to dismantle some of his strongholds and layers over unmet needs and unresolved issues. "J" was very fearful of being vulnerable, but he wanted to be free so badly that he was willing to take a major step of trust this night.

We helped "J" initiate his own freedom by leading the words of his beginning prayers, as he was unsure of what to do. As he prayed, a deep sobbing began to come up from within him and I stilled everyone while God took over. About fifteen minutes later, feeling somewhat overwhelmed but happy, "J" was pulling himself together when I had to leave the room. Returning, I found "Q" telling "J" about something else he needed to expose. "Q" had a sincere desire to help, but having been unable to deal with wrong feelings and fears emanating out of his own unhealed hurt, he was pushing for a resolution of an identical area in "J's" life.

I immediately recognized that "J" was feeling attacked while defenseless. I quickly and firmly turned the meeting in a different direction, and shortly thereafter, the meeting ended and everyone left. Early the next morning I followed up on "J" and found that much of the victory gained the previous night before was rapidly evaporating. "J" was sincerely regretting having ever opened up. "Q's" motive had not been bad, but his timing was terrible.

"Q" was unable to minister wisely and purely when his unsurrendered soul identified and reacted to an unhealed hurt in the voluntarily vulnerable "J." It is never the right time to bring a corrective word to those who have just made themselves vulnerable in order to seek help. All too often, well-meaning but inexperienced ministers and lay people view any voluntary vulnerability as a green flag to go after more than they should. Had "Q" been listening with his spirit, he would have recognized the Holy Spirit waving red flags, and saying, *"Wrong timing, wrong motive, wrong ministry. Whoa!"*

Regardless of your desire to help, there is no assurance you will always act safely and effectively with regard to other people's souls when you have unhealed hurts in your own soul. Too many people try to minister to others through identification out of their own hurts. In the next chapter, I will go into concerns over support groups bringing hurting, needy people together to identify with each other's like hurts and needs.

Unresolved Issues

Unresolved issues are birthed when you cannot effectively process painful, confusing circumstances and situations in a positive manner. Unresolved issues in a life produce many negative behavior patterns—intolerance, criticalness, insecurity, legalism, rigidity, and perfectionism are just a few. While growing up, such a person never knew what the "rules" were, where the boundaries were, where the line was drawn, or how to avoid stepping on the wrong side of it. In himself, this person will always try, through rigidity and legalism (scriptural and personal), to create an intellectual and emotional structure where his soul feels safe. Anything that does not fit inside the perimeters of that preset structure becomes a cause for alarm.

When we have unresolved issues in our lives, the devil can pressure our souls through creating circumstances that we recognize as being similar to unresolved issues from our pasts. If we react to these frightening present-day "replays," instead of loosing the lies of their power to still control us, we can be overwhelmed with feelings of confusion, fear, and anger. To be useful to God and others, we must get the layers off these "no trespassing zones" of our souls. Until we do, God can't heal us and we remain vulnerable to Satan's pressuring of our vulnerability—with our availability to God being extremely hindered.

Unresolved Issues: Sources of Procrastination and Indecisiveness

While visiting a very close, older friend who has always found decision-making frightening, I was alone in her house for several hours one day. I noticed that a good deal of produce was going bad in her refrigerator, so I decided to surprise her by cleaning out the refrigerator and then buying some fresh produce. The friend came home unexpectedly and was quite distressed that I had discarded the extremely overripe fruit and vegetables, quickly retrieving them from the trash basket. She explained that she could make soups, stew, or sauces out of them—they shouldn't be wasted.

The following week I visited her again, arriving unexpectedly. I walked into the kitchen to find my friend cleaning out her refrigerator, throwing away the now "beyond-soup/stew/sauce" fruit and vegetables. I realized this was a perfect mini "snapshot" of her fear of making decisions. Regardless of potential consequences, she often just waited until time made the decision for her.

When a child grows up in an environment where his (or her) choices frequently seem to cross unspoken, invisible boundaries to produce negative consequences, there is no motivation to learn how to make "right" choices. To this person, no choice becomes the only safe choice. Each decision that can be avoided is viewed as a negative consequence deflected. Acts of procrastination are viewed as semi-solutions, rather than indecision. Some people choose to live their entire lives with procrastination's lower-key stress rather than the spiking of fear that a decision made might turn out to be disastrous.

Others move into a deeper form of undecisiveness as a solution to their fear of the wrong decision/bad consequence syndrome. This person chooses to ignore even urgent decisions that should be made, letting them progress to "natural" conclusions that may involve great fallout. This person would rather clean up the fallout and effect damage control after a negative, natural conclusion.

Almost anything is better than having to try to make "perfect" decisions that could avoid the damage in the first place.

Layers

The soul's bottom-line defense system is constructed out of layer upon layer of self-control, self-reliance, self-protection, self-centeredness, self-defense, self-justification, etc. These are industrial-strength layers, just as the soul intended them to be. In the natural realm, it is a fact that multiple layers of bonded wood can be much stronger than a single board of equal thickness. Multiple layers of light-weight, space-age plastics, known as composites, are much stronger than a single piece of the same plastic of an equal thickness. So, the soul protects the core of its power structure with layer upon layer of different self-protective, self-defensive mechanisms.

The layering occurs over the three main areas we have already been looking at: unmet needs, unhealed hurts, and unresolved issues. These three areas are birthed by the impact of imperfect people in our lives. The world teaches us that we must find out who these people are, what their motive was, exactly what kind of hurts they inflicted upon us, what kind of needs they created in us, and make them accountable. Then we can sue them, slander them, direct our anger at them, or even some worse things that are quite frightening.

Too often we embrace this teaching in an effort to find a logical reason or excuse to justify our own behavior patterns, attitudes, fears, and reactions to those around us. It is so futile to work this hard in order to find who is to blame for our current physical, mental, emotional, and spiritual state. The culprit is quite close, within us even— our own souls, of course.

What has happened to you in the past may have been very painful. But that pain can be neutralized and filed away as a lifeless fact that you have neither need nor desire to revisit anymore. You can choose to recognize the trauma as historical and say, "Thank you, Jesus, I'm not going there anymore!" I had a revelation about the shame and pain I felt about certain past circumstances that used to trigger almost frantic efforts on my part to meet my own needs. One day about three years ago, an exact copy of an old circumstance closed in around me that I would have formerly responded to with an old behavior pattern, and I looked it right in the face and shouted, "<u>I don't have to do that anymore!</u>"

If you insist upon clinging to every bad memory, painful thought, and offense you've ever experienced, you will never have peace, healing, or victory in your life. You will always be deceived about needing to blame someone for why you are the way you are. You will always be motivated to shift accountability away from your soul and onto someone out of your past, which is never effective for true healing. The only productive confrontation regarding past pain is to confront your own soul and dismantle its efforts to hide that pain from God. You can accomplish this through binding and loosing prayers.

You must make room for the Holy Spirit to gain access into every square inch of your soul to heal your hurts, meet your needs, and make you whole. Otherwise, whatever bitterness and unforgiveness you're packing around, whatever the neediness driving you, whatever is lacking in your life, whatever confusion and pain you feel, will ooze out of you and touch everything and everyone you get near. It doesn't matter how controlled or perfect you've tried to train yourself to be—whatever you try to hide in your soul will leak out.

Training-Wheel Prayer for Forgiveness and Freedom

Jesus, you have said that we will be forgiven as we forgive others. I know this is not an impossible commandment to fulfill, although my soul thinks it is. I loose every wrong idea and pattern of thinking I have ever entertained about what is fair and right for me. I loose every wrong attitude I have ever had towards those who have embarrassed, humiliated, or ridiculed me. I loose every wrong desire for even the smallest bit of revenge.

I bind my will to your will and your way. I know you want me to set every person free from any responsibility to me, regardless of what they have done. I will forgive, and I will let you work out the details according to your greater plans and purposes. Lord, I know that you have not asked me to do this in order to let others just walk away from their wrongful acts. But I will not seek to comfort my soul's outrage by asking you to hold others accountable. I recognize that you have commanded me to forgive so that I can walk away from the offense, refusing to receive the fallout from it any longer. Forgiveness is my door out of the never-ending loop of reliving the pain and trauma over and over, day after day. I choose to forgive and cut myself completely out of this loop. I will leave the resolution of the problem to you.

Whether or not I forgive will not affect <u>how you will deal with</u> anyone else. Whether or not I forgive will only affect <u>how you will have to deal with me.</u>

You have promised to enable and empower me to do your good will in all things as I learn the beauty and the freedom of forgiveness. I bind myself to your will regarding every person who has ever passed through my life and left footprints on my heart and wounds in my soul. I pray that you bless them, Lord, and that you meet their needs, heal their hurts, and resolve all of the unresolved issues of their lives. Extend your grace and your mercy to them, Father.

Thank you, dear Jesus, for purchasing my forgiveness and allowing me to just walk away from all of my own sin and wickedness. Thank you that you did not hold a grudge against me, nor did you ask the Father to deal with me and hold me accountable for what you had to bear in my stead. I know that this great gift from you to me is more than enough, many times over, to enable me to forgive others their petty sins and offenses against me. Lord, you are so good. I thank you for your wonderful wisdom and mercy in my life. In Jesus' name, Amen.

Keep the following explanation in mind as you continue on through the rest of the book:

- <u>Strongholds</u> keep God's truth from getting to the wrong ideas, wrong attitudes, wrong beliefs, wrong motives, and wrong patterns of thinking of the soul. This is the first level of defense against any dethroning of the unsurrendered soul's position of power.

- <u>Layers</u> keep God's grace and mercy from getting to the unmet needs unhealed hurts, and unresolved issues of the soul. This is the soul's final and bottom-line level of defense against losing its position of power.

- <u>Binding and loosing prayers</u> to loose strongholds, wrong agreements, soul-ties, and the soul's layers all weaken the kingdom of self that the unsurrendered soul has built. For every stick, stone, and layer that comes down or off, a little more room is freed up to receive mercy and grace from God.

Special Note: Because spiritual principles can seem so frustrating and abstract to those who are in bondage, I have prepared a visual aid for this teaching. This is a detailed "diagram" of the inner workings of our unsurrendered souls that keep us from having an intimate relationship with Him. This has been reproduced as a colored, laminated chart with binding and loosing prayers on the back. Many have said this chart helped them to finally understand exactly what had been happening inside of them for years. See back of book to order.

6
Relationships and Agreements

The Holy Spirit uses other people to work out impurities lodged in our souls and press out the kinks in our "relational theology." But it would be a grim world, indeed, if our only purpose to one another was to sandpaper each other's rough edges. Fortunately, God has also intended that we would bring pleasure to one another. He wants us to get together, worship together, fellowship together, pray together, and have fun together.

When you have deep, unmet needs in your life, you will generally gravitate towards and be attracted to people who will "understand you." This often is a person who has the exact same kinds of unmet needs, unhealed hurts, and unresolved issues that you have. Beware of plunging into intense relationships with those people who are eager to share their pain and "feel" yours. These relationships are fraught with hidden soulish agendas and potential soul-ties. Needy souls are always seeking ways to get their needs met, hurts healed, and issues resolved.

123

Also be prayerful and wise in relating to counselors and leaders who identify with your problem and your pain because of like experiences in their own lives. There are some who have given up fixing themselves and moved into fields where they can help fix someone else instead (both in secular positions and ministry positions). They may be quite sincere and generous in their desire to help others, but they often dispense an unhealthy mixture of spiritual and soulish advice. Unless these people are extremely self-aware and disciplined, regardless of their level of professional training, they will invariably give guidance and direction that is colored by their own areas of vulnerability.

This does not mean that you should avoid all people who are not yet whole, for that would be a most lonely and singular life. Still, you should be very cautious about relating too deeply, too quickly, with individuals you are still learning about. Never buy into the lie that an individual who seems "just like you" is a once-in-a-lifetime connection you don't dare miss. God can and will give you excellent opportunities for wonderful relational experiences when your primary relationship focus is on Him.

Agenda of Love or Need?

Relationships are usually formed around an assumption that each person will give to and receive from the relationship. Christian relationships should be based upon giving God's love to others and then receiving God's love back (hopefully from them and always from Him). The purest of human love, which flows out of the soul, rarely has a God-pure agenda. Your soul's love, generosity, self-sacrifice, kindness, and acts of caring almost always have a personal agenda involving your unmet needs, unhealed hurts, and unresolved issues— sometimes innocent, sometimes very self-centered.

If you have ever felt even slightly disappointed about a response or reaction to an act of loving kindness, generosity, or great sacrifice you extended to someone else, the reason is this: You hoped for something reciprocal—love, kindness, appreciation, praise, favor, etc., in return and you didn't get it.

God-based love, *agape* love, always has a purely divine agenda. This is the agenda that seeks the very best for another person even if it means personal sacrifice. This agenda is rooted in and growing out of divine love already received. This love has no expectations and continues to grow even when it is rejected, abused, or betrayed by the one it is focused upon. It flows from God's Spirit through man's spirit into man's soul, where it is then mentally and emotionally, as well as physically, manifested through words of grace and deeds of mercy. This is the only love that helps heal all broken relationships and build godly ones. And, hallelujah, you don't have to be a completed saint in order to let some of this kind of love get through you!

All of us need people to love, to be loved by, to fellowship with, to worship with, and to agree with. All of us need people to plan with, pray with, and believe with. We need the sharing, rejoicing, spiritual balancing, and creative energy that flows in such times of togetherness.

The world's answer to socializing, fun, and companionship that all humans desire can range all the way from the "no-holds-barred, head-hunting, wherever-the-action-is scene" on one hand, to the "spill-your-feelings to the 'safe'-but-wounded-group scene" on the other hand, with many less extreme examples in between. A sense of social interaction, a sense of receiving "love," and belonging can be temporarily created, but these are not places where healthy bonds of agenda-free love are formed. These are the places where games and agendas are often played out in a fruitless pursuit of lasting peace and happiness—always at the greatest expense of those who do not understand the constantly shifting rules.

God so wants His unlimited gift of forgiveness and agenda-free love available to whoever wants to receive it. If He cared enough to send His only begotten Son to earth to die on the Cross so we could receive this gift, how can any of us think that He would withhold any part of such a gift from us? If God wants us to be instruments of healing to the world, how can we ever think He will not heal us, too? We may have been cracked and abused vessels cast by the roadside of the world until He reached out to us with His love, but He will not withhold anything from us that is necessary for our healing and wholeness now.

Natural man does not understand this unconditional, unending supply of loving mercy and restoration healing—so natural man continues to seek answers from within himself and from other humans. Other people cannot permanently fix our brokenness, nor can we permanently fix theirs. Some may be willing to distract us from our brokenness or temporarily compensate for it, as we may be willing to do for them. Others may refuse to help in any way, avoiding any chance of being blamed for the pain. But no one but the One who loves us most can truly "fix" us.

Releasing Your Imperfect People

We're not strong enough, smart enough, or brave enough in our own power to break all of our ties to the wrong teachings and unresolved circumstances that our unsurrendered souls use to "explain" why we are the way we are. Each one of us has acquired wrong beliefs from the actions of imperfect people who have left the imprint of their imperfections upon our souls. Those imperfect people had imperfect people do the same thing to them. If we do not know how to break the bondage cycle of this infectious imperfection, we repeat the same mistakes and go on to produce imperfect people when we pass through their lives.

We must stop blaming the imperfect people, stop rationalizing our reactive behaviors, and begin to live our lives according to God's truth and counsel. It doesn't matter what people have done _to_ us in the light of what has God done _for_ us. I remember one Christian woman trying to justify doing something that was clearly not scriptural, saying, "I'll be talked about if I do and talked about if I don't. So, what does it matter?" I reminded her that what really matters is what God is talking about to us. We cannot just be thermometers registering the spiritual and moral temperature of those around us, we are supposed to be thermostats setting the temperature!

The burden of the baggage of the imperfect people in your life is far too heavy for you to continue to bear—always exhausting, sometimes terrifying, ever hindering and handicapping you. Be the one in your generation who takes a stand and says:

"NO MORE! I don't have to be imperfect anymore, for the One who is greater than all others has now passed

into my life. He is wiping away all of the imperfect imprints of everyone and everything else I've ever known. I will not live under the influence of imperfect people anymore, and I will not produce any more imperfect people, either. Only blessings, grace, and mercy will come out of me from now on!"

Forgiveness Is the Catalyst of Miracles

When you became a Christian, you may have been shocked to learn that God wants you to forgive every person who has ever negatively impacted your life. Perhaps you attempted to obey this directive from the human resources within yourself. Man's natural resources for extending grace and mercy are extremely limited, if not non-existent at times; but let us assume you made the effort, anyway. Your pastor and other Christians probably encouraged you to set your will to forgive, saying that God would honor your effort and give you the grace to make it so.

That is where the process may have broken down. God will give you all grace and mercy to reach out and forgive others if you have room within yourself to receive forgiveness, grace, and mercy from Him. But existing strongholds, walls, resentments, judgments, unforgiveness, etc., in your soul creates clutter that clogs up your capacity to receive. They are "high things" that exalt themselves between you and the knowledge of how to work with God (2 Cor. 10:5, KJV). This is why 2 Corinthians 10:3-4 (AMP) tells us, *"For though we walk [live] in the flesh (flesh: the earthly nature of man apart from divine influence, i.e., the unsurrendered soul), we are not carrying on our warfare according to the flesh and using mere human weapons* (our souls' resources). *For the weapons of our warfare are not physical (weapons of flesh and blood), but they are mighty before God for the overthrow and destruction of strongholds."*

Only by using God's divine weapons can you destroy the strongholds around and the layers over your unforgiveness and your pain in order to receive a cleansing flow of His healing mercy. There is no limit to or rationing of His freely given forgiveness, love, and grace. His miraculous resources are limited only by the size and amount of space you've created within yourself to receive them.

Making Room For Miracles

In 2 Kings 4:2-7 (NIV), we read of a prophet's widow who was about to lose her two sons to a life of servitude in order to satisfy her deceased husband's unpaid creditors. She implored the prophet Elisha to help her, and when he questioned her, he learned that all she had was a little oil. So he said, " *'Go around and ask all your neighbors for empty jars. Don't ask for just a few. Then go inside and shut the door behind you and your sons. Pour oil into all the jars, and as each is filled, put it to one side.'* . . . *When all the jars were full, she said to her son, 'Bring me another one.' But he replied, 'There is not a jar left.' Then the oil stopped flowing."* This woman set the limits of her own miracle by the space she created to receive it—this was accomplished through action on her part!

Have you ever believed God for a miracle of restoration between you and another person if you put action to your faith—only to have your personal olive branch rejected? That does hurt! You believed God would show right up as soon as you reached out and everything would be gloriously resolved—sort of like a director's cry of: "Okay, lights up—now begin rolling the camera—and now cue the symphony—an-n-n-n-d ACTION!" When it didn't happen that way, you were probably told it just wasn't God's timing yet.

So often we explain away what we don't understand by spiritualizing that an undesired outcome to an act of our faith happened because it wasn't God's perfect timing yet. <u>God's timing is always a lot more "right now" than we realize.</u> The error factor you were not aware of was that <u>you had God's power, mercy, and grace blocked out</u> of the situation because of the strongholds and walls in your soul. No lights, no camera, no symphony, wrong REACTION! Trying to obey God's commandment to forgive, you went in your own limited forgiveness and grace. You may have expended a year's worth on that one scenario!

You didn't understand your need to first obey the commandment that would have opened your soul to an impartation of God's unlimited restoration resources before you went to the other person. If you had understood, you would have torn down the strongholds and vain imaginations in your soul that strengthened the high things between you and the knowledge of how to cooperate with God. You only had your little bucketful of love and grace to pour on the other person and it didn't even begin to put out the fire of his anger, defensiveness, and pain! You needed gallons and gallons of God's love and grace to float him above his wrong feelings. You can't float someone in a bucket!

Perhaps you're thinking, "Hey, I tried to do the right thing. I meant well!" Yes, you did want to do right and God wanted to respond with a miracle—but the walls of your strongholds prevented agreement between your act of faith and God's miracle response. That's the bad news. The good news is that God is waiting to come into agreement with you now and see the miracle come to pass yet!

Isn't There An Easier Way, God?

God often uses serious things we don't understand when He is trying to stretch our faith. Faith may come by reading the Word, but faith grows by acting on the Word. If you are not voluntarily stepping out to act on His Word, God will stretch you out onto it. If this is the only way He can get your faith to grow, He will use circumstances and other people to see that it happens.

Your comfort zone will never accurately register your faith's reality level so as to let you know whether or not you're growing. Any reality check issued on your comfort zone's bank will generally bounce! I've heard so many say, "My faith is just fine when everything is all right. It's only when things start falling apart that my faith falls apart." That is so silly! We don't need to use our faith when everything is going all right. Easy, good times are wonderful, and I'll get in line any day for all I can get of them. <u>But good times and blessings don't produce the unshakable, rock-solid kind of faith that comes out of standing on God's Word when everything seems to be disintegrating around you.</u> Coming through times of testing and trial with your eyes on Jesus, your peace in place, and your hopes intact, is truly a priceless experience. These times are the results of your faith being purified by fire, just like fine gold!

All too often we are tempted to pray soulish prayers during our tough times. What is a soulish prayer? It thinks good, sounds good, feels good, and your soul sees how it could be very beneficial (especially for you) if it was answered: "O God, give my husband/wife/son/daughter/ brother/mother-in-law a better attitude, so I don't have to listen to their griping. O God, send money so I don't have to wonder how my bills are going to get paid. O God, don't let anyone put any pressure on me, so I can feel your peace." And this one: "God, if you don't want me to be afraid of the devil, then make him stop scaring me!"

In other words, "God, don't make me have to believe for anything I don't have, and I'll trust you completely. Just give me everything I need as soon as I think I need it, and I promise I'll have faith in you all the time." Do you honestly think that God is going to agree with this?

The Power of Agreement

Real faith—unshakable faith—requires involvement and action with God and His Word. After frequent references in the Old Testament about Abraham's belief in God, Paul (in Romans and Galatians) and James remind their readers that <u>Abraham believed God</u>. The original Greek for the words "Abraham believed" (which resulted in him being counted as righteous before God) in Galatians 3:6 (AMP) means Abraham's belief <u>was in conformity with God's will in his every purpose, thought, and action</u>. His spirit's purpose was to believe God's words, his soul's thoughts were to be about God's greatness and faithfulness, and his body's actions were to physically correspond with his belief that God was always right.

To believe is more than just a mental assent to the words of the Bible. There are too many Christians today who say, "I believe in the Bible, it's just not working for me." That's like staring at your home computer and saying, "I believe in my computer, it's just not working for me," when you haven't even turned it on! God expects us to have purpose, think thoughts, and take action in a fully integrated expression of our beliefs. If we can't do that, then we need to confront and challenge what we "say" we believe.

Suppose you watched a man successfully carry someone back and forth on a tightrope over Niagara Falls. Then he said to you, "Do you believe I can do that again?" You said you did. "Then," he said, "this time let me carry you over the falls on my shoulders." Your affirmation of belief could no longer be just mental and verbal assent. You would have to recant your statement of belief or become directly involved—body, soul, and spirit—in acting out what you professed to believe. You need to insist that <u>your body, your soul, and your spirit are all in agreement with what you say and think you believe</u>. You need to come into agreement within your own "troops."

The Power in Wrong Agreement

There is a universal power in any form of agreement—right or wrong. In Genesis 11:1-6 (KJV), we find that, *"The whole earth was of one language, and of one speech . . . . And they* (a certain people) *said, Go to, let us build us a city and a tower, whose top may reach unto heaven; and let us make us a name, lest we*

133

be scattered abroad upon the face of the whole earth. And the Lord came down to see the city and the tower, which the children of men builded. And the Lord said, Behold, the people is one, and they have all one language and this they begin to do: and now nothing will be restrained from them, which they have imagined to do."

These were <u>not</u> born-again, regenerated people of God. They were unregenerated, ungodly people. These people, acting in one accord, set out to climb up into God's face and attempt who knows what? God said that nothing they set out to do would be impossible to them because they were able to verbally agree with each other. He then divided their speech into many different languages to keep them from being able to come into wrong agreement.

Wrong agreements always produce wrong consequences. Consider the people in Matthew 27:19-25 who cried out in agreement for the crucifixion of Jesus even as Pilate wanted to release Him. The people screamed and shouted with one voice for His crucifixion, rejecting Pilate's attempts to warn them not to do it (vss. 23-24). In one accord, they cried, *"His blood be on us, and on our children!"* (Matt. 27:25, KJV). They were in agreement with hell itself that day, and their children reaped the fruit of their wrong agreement. Less than forty years later (one generation), Roman soldiers under Titus destroyed Jerusalem and cut its inhabitants into pieces with their swords.

Agreeing With One Another

In Matthew 18:20, we read of two or three being *"gathered together"* in Jesus' name. This does not mean

134

sitting side-by-side in a church pew or in a prayer meeting. The Greek word translated as "gathered together" is *sunago* which comes from two other Greek words: *sun* meaning "together and completeness" and *ago* meaning "to lead, to draw, to bring into, or to induce." So, the two or three who are *"gathered together"* in His name in verse 20 are people who have been drawn or led by His Spirit into togetherness and completeness with Jesus, who is always in agreement with God's will. Any prayer coming out of such agreement is going to be answered by the Father every time.

Praying in agreement with people who have been led, brought, or induced to come together by any influence other than the Holy Spirit's can be both ineffective and potentially dangerous at the same time. (See soul-ties in Chapter 7.) This sheds light on why some "prayers of agreement" fail to manifest the answers we desire, even though we have invoked this verse as the basis of praying together. Whenever you're not being led by the Holy Spirit, you can convince yourself and others to agree on perfectly logical things that God is not any part of. Being *"gathered together"* in agreement must be done by the Holy Spirit to invoke the principle Jesus gave in Matthew 18:19 (NIV), *"I tell you that if two of you on earth agree about anything you ask for, it will be done for you by my Father in heaven."*

If you gather to pray according to any will other than God's and expect a Matthew 18:19 response, it won't happen. It won't matter if you're praying "in Jesus' name" or not. A Matthew 18:19 response will come only to those "gathered together" by the Holy Spirit, as in Matthew 18:20. When He gathers people together to pray, they always pray the Father's will.

135

Power is released when you bind your will to God's will because you have set your will in a position of agreement with His will. You come into agreement with God, with His Word, with His Spirit, and with all of heaven when you do that. In effect, you're in right agreement with the Lord's Prayer as well: *"Thy will be done, in earth, as it is in heaven."* We're talking about tapping into and aligning ourselves with some serious power here!

Praying in Unity

In Acts 4, we read that the priests, guards, and Sadducees had just put Peter and John in jail. These two men were not espousing personal doctrine, trying to start a church, trying to raise funds for overseas crusades; they were simply preaching the name of Jesus, which seriously rattled the religious leaders. The leaders commanded Peter and John to stop, threatened them, but then let them go. Peter and John went back to their own people and reported what had been said to them: *"And being let go, they went to their own company, and reported all that the chief priests and elders had said unto them. And when they* [the believers] *heard that, they lifted up their voice to God with one accord, and said, Lord, thou art God, which hast made heaven, and earth, and the sea, and all that in them is"* (Acts 4:23-24, KJV).

The believers, upon hearing the report of Peter and John, began to lift up their voices as in one accord, quoting from the holy Scriptures (Psalm 146:6, KJV). Continuing on from verse 29 through verse 31: *"And now, Lord, behold their threatenings: and grant unto thy servants, that with all boldness they may speak thy word, by stretching forth thine hand to heal; and that signs*

and wonders may be done by the name of thy holy child
Jesus. And when they had prayed, the place was shaken
where they were assembled together; and they were all
filled with the Holy Ghost, and they spake the word of
God with boldness. And the multitude of them that
believed <u>were of one heart and of one soul</u>" (KJV).

These Christians were in agreement, all praying
from the Word of God. That is sometimes the only way
some Christians come into one accord, because we're all
so diverse in our minds, wills, and emotions.

There was a time during the eighties when it was
considered prideful to say, "Lord, <u>I</u> pray—<u>I</u> command—
<u>I</u> rebuke—." Instead, you would hear Christians pray,
"Lord, <u>we</u> believe—<u>we</u> rebuke—<u>we</u> command—." I
began to wonder about those who were being included
in this prayer of agreement who <u>weren't in one accord</u>
with what was being prayed. In Acts 16:18 (AMP), Paul
was sorely annoyed and worn out from the slave girl
(being possessed by a spirit of divination) who kept
following him, shouting loudly. Finally, he *"turned and*
said to the spirit within her, <u>I</u> charge [I command, KJV)
you in the name of Jesus to come out of her! And it came
out that very moment."

I remember one particular morning service in a
small church I attended in the mid-eighties where
everything in the world seemed to be disrupting the
flow—children were crying, teenagers were going back
and forth to the bathrooms, adults were coughing and
sneezing. The pastor kept praying over and over, "Lord,
in Jesus' name, we command the devil to leave this
service," but nothing happened. Finally, thoroughly
frustrated, he happened to look at me and said, "Liberty,
will you take authority over this confusion?"

Before I could think about what I was going to say (I wasn't brave enough to pray binding and loosing prayers in public yet), I stood up and blurted out, "Father, in the name of Jesus Christ, I command every wrong spirit to leave this building right now!" The church went totally silent and not another peep or squeak was heard for the duration of the pastor's message. However, I was uncomfortably aware of great disapproval from some who felt I had prayed a prideful prayer. Whether I was right in what I did or not, I learned something important that day.

Because of the varying levels of experience, understanding, faith, and involvement of that diversified body on any given day, there was no way of knowing if everyone would be in corporate agreement with rebuking or commanding anything. We can't possibly expect to be in one accord with one another if we are all determining God's will out of our own experiences and feelings during any given day.

God's Spirit alone can draw us into perfect unity. Binding our wills to His will, making room for His will to be fulfilled through us, we will receive His unifying help. Binding ourselves to an awareness of the power of the blood that makes us one brings us into unity. By binding our minds to the mind of Christ, we come into unity with the Head of our corporate Body. Only when I am with a group that understands binding and loosing prayer principles do I ever use the corporate pronoun "we" in this way: "*Lord, we bind ourselves, everyone else who is involved, and this situation to your will and purposes. We loose all hindrances and devices of the enemy from ourselves, all who are involved, and this situation.*"

Agreeing With God

There is enormous power in coming into one accord with other people, but there is greater power when you come into agreement with God himself. In Exodus 25, God told builders to put a solid gold mercy seat over His ark and to put the testimony of His Word into the ark. Then He told Moses in Exodus 25:22, *"And there I will meet with thee, and I will commune with thee from above the mercy seat..."* (KJV). The phrase *"meet with thee"* in this verse comes from the Hebrew word *ya`ad,* which means "agreement." This is the same word used in Amos 3:3, *"Can two walk together, except they be agreed?"* God was saying that the place of agreement was where He would meet with us. God will walk with us, meet with us, and communicate with us in the place of agreement right between His Word and His mercy.

There have been times when I have felt I couldn't hear a word of communion from God. Was God being silent? Sometimes. But more than likely, I missed our meeting place—the only place where believers will ever be able to come together in one accord and agree with God and with each other. How many times have we blown getting to the right meeting place—in His Word? Every time our souls kicked up their heels, I'll bet. This is one place a stubborn, willful soul definitely does not want to go.

Missing the Meeting

When you try to read the Word and come into a place of agreement with God, have you ever felt that your mind is leaping around like a drop of water on a hot griddle while your feelings begin acting like a fourteen year old's hormones? The kids, the dog, the cat, and the neighbor's power mower all cut loose at once as soon as you attempt to "get spiritual." Let me tell you why. Your unsurrendered soul and Satan's evil spirits swing into action in order to stop you from going into that meeting place with God because they know they can't go in with you.

God <u>will work through</u> a surrendered soul, but God <u>will actually meet with</u> your regenerated spirit. Wow! Whatever spiritual blessing your emotions and mind feel from the presence of God are from the overflow of your spirit.

God Will Not Be Mocked

Galatians 6:7 (KJV) says, *"Be not deceived; God is not mocked: for whatsoever a man soweth, that shall he also reap."* I originally thought this verse referred to unbelievers, backsliders, and hypocrites. Then I read the same verse in *The Amplified Bible*, on the same day God decided it was time for me to quit kidding myself in a couple of areas. *The Amplified Bible* says this: *"Do not be deceived and deluded and misled; God will not allow himself to be sneered at—scorned, disdained or mocked [by mere pretensions or professions, or by His precepts being set aside]—He inevitably deludes himself who attempts to delude God. For whatever a man sows, that and that only is what he will reap."* Don't ever try to fool God or yourself about whether or not you are in agreement with Him in every area of this verse!

When I really began to study this verse about three years ago, I checked my heart for mere pretensions of faith or obedience. I felt that I wasn't trying to <u>pretend</u> to be more faithful or obedient than I was. Then I checked out mere professions I might be making, but I'm pretty open about most of my shortcomings (or "tallcomings," as the case may be). I didn't think I was <u>professing</u> to be something other than what I think I actually am. Two out of three—so far so good, I thought.

Then I got to the part about setting aside God's <u>precepts</u>. My spirit started convicting and my soul started justifying—I knew from the general "Keystone Cops Scramble" that ensued, I was onto something. Do not deceive yourself, says the Word of God. Do not try to set God's precepts aside. Whatsoever you sow, you will reap. This also works the other way as well, whatsoever you don't sow, you won't reap. That's when I went **beyond** the binding and loosing, because they had done their job to bring me to the place of receiving new truth. I began to repent as the Holy Spirit began to show me why there seemed to be a drought in my life at that time.

For nearly two years, my phone had been ringing off the hook about this "new" binding and loosing revelation God had given me. Everyone had questions, needed prayer, wanted advice, wanted Scriptures, wanted to talk to me. I got phone calls late at night, I got them early in the morning, I got them while I was trying to eat. I got them while I was trying to watch television. I got them while I was in the shower. I began to mentally monitor people's calls, thinking, "Okay, you've already called me twice in the last five days. That's enough. I don't have any more time for you this week." I began to let my answering machine pick up my calls. I began to resent the phone ringing at all!

As this continued for months, I kept getting more and more frustrated over it. I was constantly being interrupted when I was trying to meet this or that deadline and get to Federal Express. So I would talk or pray quickly and get people off the phone. I began to complain to friends and other ministers and, unfortunately, some responded with just what my soul wanted to hear: "You can't let other people consume you. You can't be their contact point to God, they have some responsibility to get their own meat. You should just turn your phone off. You can't let the people drain you or you won't be any good to anybody, etc., etc., etc." That all sounded pretty logical and good to me.

Then, one day, the phone stopped ringing. People stopped asking me to pray for them. People stopped calling me to come for ministry engagements. Incoming finances stopped. My publisher stopped finding work for me to do. <u>Everything stopped</u>. It was during this period of time that God confronted me with this Scripture. *"Do not be deceived and deluded and misled. God will not allow himself to be sneered at—scorned, disdained or mocked by mere pretensions or professions, or His precepts being set aside! He inevitably deludes himself who attempts to delude God. For whatever a man sows, that and that only is what he will reap."*

I became very aware that God had given me opportunity after opportunity, month after month (that's grace!), to sow help and hope and encouragement and prayer into people's lives on a very simple level. He had given me a wonderful blessing in the understanding of *Shattering Your Strongholds* and I was finding it "inconvenient" to share it one-on-one in my everyday life. I wanted people to read my book and come to my conferences and classes, but not to call my home. I wanted to be left alone there—I wanted some privacy. So God gave it to me.

Right about the same time, God also confronted me with Galatians 6:2-4 (AMP), *"Bear (endure, carry) one another's burdens and troublesome moral faults, and in this way fulfill and observe perfectly the law of Christ, the Messiah, and <u>complete what is lacking in your obedience to it</u>. For if any person thinks himself to be somebody [too important to condescend to shoulder another's load], when he is nobody [of superiority except in his own estimation], he deceives and deludes and cheats himself. But let every person carefully scrutinize and examine and test his own conduct and his own work...."* Ouch!

I was so focused on what I was doing that I felt I didn't have time to sow single seeds of encouragement when God gave me opportunities to do so. I believed that it simply wasn't productive to spend fifteen minutes at a time on the phone with only one individual—several times each day. So, by not sowing individually when I could avoid it and by resenting sowing individually when I couldn't avoid it, I allowed my own fields of harvest to become fallow—and I poisoned my own well. But God gave me the privacy I wanted.

If you had asked me if I was in the will of God during that time, I would have said I was. I was doing what needed to be done, what was obviously "there" for my hands to do. I was "making tents" like Paul did by working for my publisher. I was teaching classes once a week, continuing to study, and pressing on with my intercessors' group every Tuesday. It made sense to me that I had deadlines to meet and I was too busy to take several phone calls a day. I always prayed for people and ministered to them when I was at a meeting—often for hours. Wasn't that enough?

143

I felt justified, verified, and clarified—sanitized, even. I was "in the right." But there is no being "in the right" as a Christian, there is only being "in the Way"—His way.

After I had received God's revelation of my lack of compassion and love for the many individuals who were hungry for this new understanding, I repented and God began to restore me. Would you believe the phone rang again the next morning at 7:30? The person who called probably couldn't believe that I would pour out such prayer and encouragement and blessings at that hour of the morning. I had many, many opportunities after that to sow into individual lives and, as I did so joyfully, God regulated the calls perfectly.

Shortly thereafter, I had a pre-dawn phone call from a lady clear across the U.S.(three hours later) who had just received a copy of my book. I spent nearly thirty minutes on the phone with her, answering questions and explaining details about this concept, then praying for her. At the end of the call, she said she had received my book in the mail with a tape-of-the-month from a large, well-known ministry in another state. I called this ministry to thank them and found myself transferred from person to person in the office who wanted to thank me for what my book had meant to them. Two weeks later, I was called by the pastor's wife and asked if I would fly in and speak at their annual women's conference.

Exactly what am I saying? I doubt if I would have had any of the wonderful experiences I've reaped over the last few years, had I not recognized that I was setting God's precepts aside in favor of honoring my own ministry/work schedules. *"For if any person thinks himself to be somebody [too important to condescend to shoulder another's load], when he is nobody [of superiority except in his own estimation], he deceives and deludes and cheats himself."*

Obedience to God's principles and precepts go hand-in-hand with the promises He gives to you. We tend to equate sowing and reaping with tithes and offerings. But it applies to <u>anything you have</u> that you can sow into another's life—blessings, time, encouragement, opening of doors, giving help. I've never forgotten hearing Iverna Tompkins say that when people ask her if they can have a copy of her sermon notes after she has just preached a stirring message, she always says, "Of course you can." She learned a long time ago that the more you are willing to share and give away, the more you have sown into a return harvest in your own ministry.

Whenever God gives you a revelation of something that is strong and good and you begin to share it with others, then more revelation comes. And as you share that, more comes. Why should God keep pouring new revelation into a vessel that only wants to store it up and leak out a drop here and there? God says to give, and it will come back to you—pressed down, shaken together, and running over. (See Luke 6:38.)

7

Soul Power and Soul-Ties

God created Adam's body out of the dust of the ground and then He breathed life (or spirit) into him. When that occurred, Genesis says that man became a living soul. The spirit and the soul of a man are totally different entities—one belongs to God, the other "belongs" to man. Your spirit is God-conscious, your soul is self-conscious. Your body is earth/environment-conscious. Your soul is the control tower between the natural world your body relates to and the supernatural world your spirit relates to. When unsurrendered, it chooses which world you will most identify with.

Adam obviously had tremendous intellectual power before his fall. He was told in Genesis 2 to take care of the entire Garden of Eden (which was probably much, much larger than we think), to dress it and to keep it, and to have dominion over every living creature in it. The ability to organize and implement all of this responsibility was inherent in his soul. This astounding ability and power in Adam's soul was like a magnet to Satan. Satan has always initiated his works of darkness through the souls of men and women. Whenever he successfully tempts your soul into agreement with him, your body will eventually manifest related physical responses and actions. Sin is the natural outcome of any "dialogue" between the unsurrendered soul and the devil.

Where Did the Soul's Original Power Go?

After the Fall, when Adam's spirit suffered separation from God, I believe God diminished Adam's ability to use the formerly accessible capabilities of his soul. Watchman Nee says God did not remove these abilities from mankind's souls, He just made them latent ("hidden, escaping notice, inactive, having a dormant potential"). Rather than destroying these super-abilities, God sunk them deep into the internal being of man, immobilizing or "freezing" them.

For the most part, man has not figured out how to tap into but a little of the potential of that latent power. Through extremely focused meditation practices designed to reach within man's soul, some have gone deeper than others. Many cults and "religions" exist just to teach this form of introspective rummaging around in the unsurrendered soul's subconscious. Men and women who have caused great destruction and loss of lives through their ability to control others—Jezebel, Hitler, Jim Jones, David Koresh, etc.,—knew how to use soul power. Satan is more than ready to assist you in drawing upon your soul's latent power, for any soul power released through man's own efforts will always be used for wrong reasons.

Why Hasn't God Done Something?

We can see the power of the soul operating in the world today. Man has already learned to do clever and deceptive things through this human source of power. I believe most of the paranormal things we hear about today—psychics, divination, bending and moving of objects, mental telepathy, etc.,—begin through a utilization of soul power. Paranormal happenings usually end up being mixed with demonic power, but they begin in the soulish realm.

Why didn't God just wipe out the power potential of the soul when man fell? Wouldn't that have simplified life on earth, making us all of equal weakness, so to speak? God has purposes for the soul that have not yet been fully revealed. I believe this latent power of the soul will be dramatically brought to the forefront in the end times in a way that the world does not understand. It will be in a manner that many Christians will not really understand, either.

God is going to reveal such revelation and power through His believers' spirits in these final days that their souls (minds, wills, and emotions) will have to be mega-powerful in order to implement the natural expressions and manifestations resulting from this outpouring. The world will need a "translation" or "interpretation" of what will take place once God starts the outpouring. The "translators" or "interpreters" will be the strong, transformed, renewed and divinely released minds, wills, and emotions of His people.

We need to recognize that God's power is not just going to be flashing, crashing, and thundering around "out there" somewhere. This last-days outpouring of His power is not just going to cause buildings to fall, mountains to tumble, and rivers to run upstream. God's power is also going to be manifested through His people, causing believers' words to stop storms, raise the dead, and calm hungry wild beasts. God's power is also going to cause believers' hands to impart healing, their minds to impart divine knowledge, and their wills to set courses that man has never yet walked. Just imagine, the God of eternity will be pouring supernatural power and knowledge into regenerated spirits to be manifested in the natural through the surrendered souls and bodies of Christians here on earth. What a concept!

The Commission of the Human Soul

My mind reels at some of the rapidly evolving social, economic, and technological trends of today. It tips into overload whenever input comes from several of these sources at once. Unless I'm upgraded, translated, or "angelicated," I know my finite human abilities will never be able to receive and manifest what God is going to pour out in the near future. I believe God is going to bring the latent power of souls "on-line" in His believers, and their surrendered souls are going to become divinely-driven "vehicles" of expression of what our spirits receive from Him.

According to the prophet Daniel, the Old Testament's counterpart and link to the apostle John in the Book of the Revelation, much power and wisdom and knowledge will be available to those who know their God in the final age of the Church. Daniel was speaking prophetically of the end-time Church when he wrote the words recorded in Daniel 11:32-33 (AMP), " . . . *The people who know their God shall prove themselves strong and shall stand firm, and do exploits [for God]. And they who are wise and understand among the people shall instruct many and make them understand . . . .* " Then in 12:3-4, 10 (AMP), Daniel's words reveal, *"And the teachers and those who are wise shall shine like the brightness of the firmament; and those who turn many to righteousness—to uprightness and right standing with God [shall give forth light] like the stars for ever and ever . . . many shall run to and fro and search anxiously [through the Book], and knowledge [of God's purposes as revealed by His prophets] shall be increased and become great . . . none of the wicked shall understand, but the teachers and those who are wise shall understand. "*

Many Seeking Soul Power

There are many cultures, groups, and "religions" trying to release the power within the soul of man. Some teachings are directed at disciplining and punishing the body, some at uniting the body and soul, some at strengthening the soul to transcend the body. Regardless of the "spiritual" language involved, these teachings all have a single governing principle: break through all physical and material bonds and release the latent power of the soul.

Revelation 18:13 says that in the last days, men's souls will become as merchandise. What can that mean? Does it actually mean that people's souls can be bought or hired to provide increased power for ungodly purposes? Think of the hundreds of thousands of Muslims who pray daily (all at the same time) towards Mecca.

Muslims are not regenerated, born-again believers in Jesus Christ. I believe their prayers, therefore, are prayers from souls that are not surrendered to God's divine purposes. Think of the multiplied power of those soulish prayers, all prayed in one accord. Muslims might be deceived about the one true God, but they do know that if you want to get something accomplished, you get multitudes of people to agree to "pray" the same thing over and over every day. Not just on Sunday and during Wednesday night prayer meetings!

The Christian's Deception

I have been completely deceived a few times in Christian "settings" in the last few years, all because something that seemed right appealed to my soul. It is getting harder and harder to recognize some of the shades of off-white and pale gray in the soulish realm these days. Your unsurrendered soul can rationalize these "shadings" so cleverly that only by knowing how to separate between soul and spirit can you discern the truth. This "knowing" is not a product of just scriptural reading, hearing, or praying. It will only come from consistently <u>doing</u> what you've read, heard, and received from the Holy Spirit in response to your seeking. This discerning or knowing comes to those "... *whose senses and mental faculties are <u>trained by practice to discriminate and distinguish</u> between what is morally good and noble and what is evil and contrary either to divine or human law*" (Heb. 5:14, AMP).

It will not be the heavy metal music, the bars, the drug dealers, the pornography, or the violence of today that will take down some believers when things get really intense in these last days. It will be the carnal believers' helplessness before the enormous soul power many people are learning to fine-tune to be used for manipulating human minds, wills, and emotions. Many Christians today are lulled into a state of complacency that all is well with their souls and their spiritual lives because they go to church and sing and praise and "amen" the message.

But many lukewarm Christians are in the same dangerous state today of the proverbial "frog in the pan" in the laboratory experiment. Put a frog into a pan of nice climate-controlled water, enhance the pan to look like his favorite environment, play a tape of sounds he recognizes, and give him a nice little padded pew of gravel to sit on. Then begin to raise the temperature of the water around him one degree at a time, and the frog will adapt his body temperature, one degree at a time, to the slowly increasing temperature. That frog will <u>sit right there</u> and adapt until it is boiled alive! Hello?

The Mystery of Iniquity

Christians are adapting to the increase of the mystery of iniquity at work in the world today—degree-by-degree, it has already begun to happen. Which one of us isn't already shock-proofed to some of the evil around us? Which one of us hasn't said, "Well, compared to some of the other movies/books/music/language/behavior, etc., around today, this isn't as bad as it could be." If you won't admit that you've said that, I will admit that I have. And finding myself saying it, I realized that what I was passing off as "not as bad as it could be" would have <u>fried my sensibilities</u> twenty-five years ago! This process of gradual desensitization to iniquity is everywhere.

The mystery of iniquity (2 Thess. 2:7 KJV) has been at work for some time: *"For the mystery of iniquity doth already work: only he who now letteth will let, until he be taken out of the way."* Many have believed that this means the full force of the mystery of iniquity would not be released until the Holy Spirit *(he who now letteth)* was taken from earth. This *"taking out of the way"* is most often believed to mean when the Church is taken away (or raptured), with a corresponding belief that the Holy Spirit will leave the earth at the same time. He is not going to do that. If the Holy Spirit left mankind when the Church is taken, who would draw those to Christ who get saved after the rapture? Who would anoint, empower, and work with those who witness to men and women after the Church is taken?

I believe 2 Thessalonians 2:7 is telling us that the Holy Spirit will be instructed to step aside, no longer holding back the full impact of the mystery of iniquity while <u>the Church is still here</u>. I can remember hearing many ministers say in years past that we would not have to worry about the Tribulation—the unleashed full force of the mystery of iniquity, the terrible things of the last days—because we would be gone. Hallelujah, we were going to be raptured and miss it all! I can also remember wanting to believe that, but always feeling a little queasy about these statements.

For the record: I'm not a card-carrying member of the pre-trib, mid-trib, or post-trib crowds. I have never been too concerned about where I fit into that end-time schedule. There are some things I just don't get now, don't need to, and probably won't until eternity. God's ways and thoughts are so far above my understanding, I'm just <u>focusing on making room to receive</u> whatever

He decides I should know, whenever. I just want to be fully able to function with unction from above, whatever "trib" position I land in!

Christian Soul Power Is Going To Be Exposed

There are people in the church world, as well as outside of it, who are used to functioning through the power of their souls. There are even some in the Body of Christ today who are aware that their soul power is enhanced whenever another soul comes into wrong agreement with them. If you are not aware of this, there is a very real risk of your being caught up into a soul-tie with others—once again, in the church world as well as outside of it. God's people are called to be one in spirit, with husbands and wives also being one in flesh with each other. No one is called to be one in soul. There is no such thing as a good soul-tie.

There are many soul-powered, high-energy Christian meetings taking place across the nation today. Those who conduct these meetings are filling the seats and packing the believers in like sardines. There are some television ministries operating in a like manner and style. There are some church services being conducted in this same way. Most of the ministers conducting these meetings sincerely believe they are operating in the best of intentions, doing what God has told them. But they are not moving in a spiritual realm; they are trying to do God's business in the soulish realm.

Some of these ministers are headed for a one-on-one confrontation with the Most High God they are "honoring" as the source of all their inspiration and direction. They love God, they are called, they have anointing, and they <u>are going to come into alignment</u> with God's plans and purposes for their end-time ministries. Many of them are going to experience some <u>serious</u> realigning of their spiritual compasses in the next few months.

We must all learn to stop responding out of our souls to the gift-wrapping of the messengers and listen intently with our spirits to the message they are offering. What is the lasting value of the gift in their messages? Did any permanent result or change come into your life after you heard the messages? Are you different, are you better in any way, has the truth of their messages remained vibrant and alive in your life months later?

Have you ever stopped to think about the fact that Jesus Christ is recorded in the written Word as pure gift, with no mention of the "gift-wrapping" of any of His physical or soulish traits? We know nothing about His height, weight, hairstyle, shape of His mouth, size of His muscles, or His personal and physical mannerisms. This is not an accident! God knew that if we were able to relate to Jesus Christ on physical or soulish terms, we would all try to copy His appearance and mannerisms. We would have churches and ministries full of little "Jesus-Ken dolls" and "Jesus-Barbie dolls." Our heavenly Father wanted us to receive and know, in a purely spiritual way, Christ as the gift of all gifts—gift-wrap not included! This is how we should receive every minister, leader, brother, and sister, as well.

Soul-Ties

In one prayer meeting I ministered at, a young girl named Jenny became confused and upset when someone gently teased her. She began to cry and then apologized profusely for being so stupid. I sensed this reaction came out of her being in wrong agreement with some word curses spoken by an authority in her life. We all agreed in prayer with her as she bound herself to the mind of Christ and the will of God and then loosed and severed any and all wrong agreements and soul-ties. She immediately felt better, the meeting ended, and we went home.

Later that afternoon Jenny called to tell me something strange had happened. At the exact time we had agreed with her prayers in one town to break the power of <u>any and all soul-ties</u> affecting her, a prayer partner in another town felt a sudden memory loss and sense of confusion. Jenny asked me if I thought she had a soul-tie with her prayer partner. Those are the moments when you need to carefully weigh your words as you concentrate on hearing the Holy Spirit. I asked Jenny if she and the other girl had ever prayed any soulish prayers together, coming into agreement over things that were not completely scriptural. Had they prayed anything she would have hesitated to pray openly in front of her whole church? They had.

Jenny and the other girl had been praying out of negative judgments and their personal opinions of the youth pastor in their church, asking God to remove him. God calls and places His leaders, and God alone should direct the removal of His leaders. Jenny and this girl had no business praying prayers in hopes of a dismissal of any leader in this church. Coming into agreement on soulish prayers had created a soul-tie between Jenny and the other girl that needed to be broken. This had happened earlier that day in the meeting, by the general loosing of "any and all" soul-ties. God had been faithful to reveal this soul-tie before any mischief of the enemy was unleashed.

Do not pray any prayers based upon personal opinions, legalistic judgments, or emotional feelings— yours or anyone else's. We will all be tempted to judge from our souls until they are completely freed from unmet needs, unhealed hurts, and unresolved issues. Perfectly impartial spiritual judges are still few and far between in the Body of Christ. So, watch out for any self-anointed, "holy" fruit inspectors hanging out in the church parking lot. Most of our prayers, and definitely most of theirs, about how God should straighten out the failures we "discern" in others are almost always soulish prayers.

A soulish prayer sounds good, feels good, and you think you know exactly how God should answer it. Praying soulish prayers in agreement with other believers who think "just like you do," can land you in a soul-tie situation with them. In rarer situations, I believe you can also come into wrong agreement with an appealing lie from an evil spirit, forming a soul-tie with it. Evil spirits don't have bodies of their own, but they do have souls— minds, wills and emotions. If you doubt that, read Ezekiel 28 about Lucifer's intelligence, determination, and pride. Stop listening with your soul, stop agreeing out of your soul, and stop praying with a soulish agenda.

David and Jonathan

I've counseled several men and women who have seemed unable to get free from unwise thoughts and unhealthy feelings and desires regarding someone they have had a close relationship with. One thing I always address in these circumstances is the breaking of soul-ties. When I first began to study soul-ties, I always referred to them as either godly or ungodly. I had been told that there were godly soul-ties, such as in marriage and in the relationship between David and Jonathan in 1 Samuel.

So I began to study 1 Samuel 18:1-3 (KJV): *"And it came to pass, when he* [David] *had made an end of speaking unto Saul, that the soul of Jonathan was knit with the soul of David, and Jonathan loved him as his own soul. And Saul took him* [David] *that day, and would let him go no more home to his father's house. Then Jonathan and David made a covenant, because he* [Jonathan] *loved him as his own soul."* When Jonathan came into this first meeting with David, he immediately desired a knitting together of their souls, and he accomplished it. David was a young man after God's own heart, anointed to be the king of Israel, yet he was able to be drawn into a wrong agreement with Saul's son, Jonathan.

We cannot tell from this scriptural record what Jonathan's hidden agenda actually was, whether he was just drawn to David's charismatic presence or whether he was thinking far ahead of that day. Perhaps he saw David replacing his father on the throne in the future, and he wanted to align himself with potential power. I personally believe Jonathan was quite devious, lining up alliances with whoever might benefit him the most. Saul was a devious king, full of soulish jealousy and paranoia. It is not hard to believe that his son would have wrong motives within his own soul, wanting to enhance his own position in the palace.

Just one chapter later, in 1 Samuel 19:1-3 (KJV), we read, *"And Saul spake to Jonathan his son, and to all his servants, that they should kill David. But Jonathan Saul's son delighted much in David: and Jonathan told*

David, saying, Saul my father seeketh to kill thee: now therefore, I pray thee, take heed to thyself until the morning, and abide in a secret place, and hide thyself: and I will go out and stand beside my father in the field where thou art, and I will commune with my father of thee; and what I see, that will I tell thee." David realized how dangerous his position was with King Saul. Instead of turning to God, because his soul was now in ascendancy over his spirit, David turned to his "soul-mate," Jonathan, for help.

David's previously quiet and innocent soul was now linked with Jonathan's strong, devious soul which acted out of the unmet needs, unhealed hurts, and unresolved issues within it. Growing up in the double-minded household of Saul would have birthed great confusion and need in any young boy's soul. Saul was double-minded because his soul's great desire to be honored, admired, and revered was in constant conflict with the spiritual truth and training given to him by God's prophet, Samuel.

In I Samuel 20:4 (KJV), Jonathan again relates intense feeling for David, *"Then said Jonathan unto David, Whatsoever thy soul desireth, I will even do it for thee."* The Hebrew word used in these verses for "soul" is *nephesh* 5315 (3c), which Gesenius generally defines to mean <u>the understanding and the faculty of thinking</u>. I believe these verses are not a confirmation or condoning of this knitting of souls as a good thing, rather they are reporting something wrong that happened. David's soul was filled with conflict from the day he met Jonathan. From his youth on, the Bible records no instances of David ever having lost his temper with anyone, having lost his peace, or having lost his assurance that God was with him—whether he was facing a lion, a bear, or a giant. Not until he met Jonathan.

David now ceased looking to God for everything God had always so graciously given to him. He became dependent instead upon drawing from the soulish resources of Jonathan, and his life began to go rapidly downhill. He slept in caves, dressed in rags, and constantly seemed to be running for his life. He finally ended up in Gath, impersonating a madman. David, anointed to be king of Israel, was so diminished in relying first upon the soulish resources of Jonathan, and then upon his own soulish resources, that he panicked when the king's servants were about to identify him. He pretended to be insane, scribbling crazily on the gates and drooling down the front of his beard and clothes. How far this man after God's own heart had fallen when reduced to surviving by his own wits!

Jonathan's Soul

I do not believe that Jonathan was a very godly person. In 1 Samuel 14, Saul swore his fighting men to an oath to abstain from food, being cursed if any of them ate before he had avenged himself of the Philistines they had just routed. The hungry army (Jonathan was with them, Saul was not) came to a place in the woods where they found a large supply of honey. None of the soldiers dared touch it because of Saul's words. But Jonathan had not heard the threat of such a curse, and he dipped his staff into the honeycomb to eat the honey. Scripture tells us that his eyes brightened, meaning that his strength was renewed.

The men were dismayed, telling him that his father had said that anyone who ate would be cursed. Jonathan coolly replied, *"My father has made trouble for the country. See how my eyes brightened when I tasted a little of this honey. How much better it would have been if the men had eaten today some of the plunder they took from their enemies. Would not the slaughter of the Philistines have been even greater?"* (1 Sam. 14:29, NIV). Jonathan criticized his father, rebelled against his command, put down his wishes, and encouraged the men to believe that they would have been better off if they had rebelled, too.

Four chapters later (in Chapter 18) David's peaceful, quiet soul came into agreement with this rebellious, disobedient, and disrespectful soul in Jonathan. After the knitting together of their souls, David's own soul began to manifest uncharacteristic, aberrant behavior patterns. Perhaps it was the first time that David's soul had been aroused, because he had been so spiritually in line with God's Spirit. Even though David still had a love for God, he began to manifest visible, external signs of the internal conflict of his soul. David was now experiencing pride, anger, deception, covetousness, and murderous thoughts. David was in a constant struggle with his soul from then on, even experiencing returns of this struggle after he turned his heart back to God.

No Such Thing as a Good Soul-Tie

Soul-ties are the product of a wrong agreement between two people. Wrong agreements usually appear to hold a promise of some kind of <u>benefit</u> for each person involved. Even if one person is seemingly forced or feels threatened into entering the wrong agreement, the "benefit" can be that something worse may have been avoided (i.e., embarrassment, loss of status, blackmail, etc.).

Several years ago, I entered into a wrong agreement with a Christian leader that produced a soul-tie that had to be broken. I succumbed to old wrong beliefs and feelings that I would be misunderstood and accused of being rebellious if I resisted agreeing with this leader who was using soul power to pressure me. I "felt I had no choice" at the time, which was not true, of course. The <u>benefit</u> I thought I saw in this wrong agreement was <u>acceptance, approval, and increased exposure on a ministry level</u>. I had "shot myself in the foot" so many times in my earlier days as an aggressive, opinionated, mouthy new Christian that I had been accused of having a "Jezebel spirit." I was deeply hurt and wounded by this accusation, and I never knew how to let go of the unresolved issues of the circumstances surrounding this accusation.

When nearly the same identical circumstance (i.e., disagreeing with a Christian leader) seemed to resurface in my life at this later date several years ago, I made a wrong choice that I believed would protect my new self-image of being submissive. I had an instant fear of being accused of being uncooperative or rebellious, of once again being labeled as having a "Jezebel spirit." This wrong choice later required me to pursue an unhappy "disengaging and untangling" mode that I knew I would never resolve satisfactorily for the other person. I simply had to apologize, get myself free, and pray that God would reveal anything further that needed to be revealed to whomever.

Satan is a master at <u>creating "copycat" circumstances to mirror the past circumstances of your "unresolved issues."</u> When difficult issues aren't resolved correctly the first time, I believe he records all of the details surrounding them and then reruns another set of them on you at a later date. The issues produced may not be resolved correctly the next time, either—unless you've experienced renewal within your soul by letting God into every area it has tried to hide.

We should never attempt to deal with our unresolved issues by just trying to sweep them into that cavernous Christian cliché known as "under the blood." If a certain issue caused you great pain, confusion, and fear, only God's grace will allow that issue to be resolved and then placed "under the blood." **The flaw in this "under the blood" Christian cliché is:** We can't put things under the blood ourselves, especially when we don't know how to let go of them in the first place. Only the grace of God can heal and resolve all issues forever.

No Such Thing as No Choice

While most wrong agreements are the by-product of expectations of getting one's own needs met, some wrong agreements can seem to be "forced." However, the statement, "I had no choice," is simply not true—whether the consequences may be as extreme as bodily harm or only slightly damaging to one's self-image and expectations. We often look at many of our tough choices through a veil of anxiety and apprehension: How am I going to be personally affected by the results of this choice? God looks at our tough choices as either a miracle-producing-process of acting by faith or a hard-trip-back-around-Mt.-Sinai-process of not acting by faith. We always have a choice in every circumstance of our own lives.

Imagine a ninety-pound Christian woman being forced against the wall of a dark alley by a three-hundred pound man holding a knife to her throat. Believe it or not, <u>she has a choice</u>.

Choice #1: Is she going to let fear explode in her soul, thereby causing her to dissolve into hysteria and stark terror? If she chooses to surrender to this choice, she will be incapable of helping herself or positively impacting her adversary in any way.

Choice #2: She can choose to immediately pray, "I bind my mind and this man's mind to the mind of Christ, and I bind my will and this man's will to your will, God. I loose fear, doubt, and all strongholds from myself and from this man. Thank you, Holy Spirit for what you are going to do."

Choice #2 is a decision to place the belief of her spirit above the fear of her soul. God has not given His children spirits that are filled with fear, rather His children's spirits are filled with power and love which produce a sound mind (2 Tim. 1:7). So, <u>there is no fear in her spirit</u>. This choice rejects anything her soul is flashing and thundering at her that contradicts what she has already settled in her spirit's understanding. By binding herself and the man to God's will, she has relinquished every detail of the resolution of this scenario to God, believing His love for her will be fulfilled for His good purposes.

Balance of Power in Soul-Ties

In a soul-tie, the soul initiating the wrong agreement is usually somewhat "stronger" than the other one. The use of the word stronger is intended to be descriptive not of the force, but of the <u>source</u> of the power drive coming out of the soul. The "stronger" soul's drive may come from a reservoir of power the person has already learned how to access and use, or it may come from a greater intensity of unmet needs and unhealed hurts seeking a solution to fear, restlessness, and pain. Either way, the stronger soul will position itself to manipulate the other soul.

Think of women who live in abusive, physically violent relationships. I have talked with some of them in crisis situations, trying to convince them to remove themselves from immediate danger until both parties can get outside help. Frequently, these women will not come out of their situations. They might say they want to, they might even try to, but something powerful compels them to return to the situation. I believe it is the power of the dominant souls (in this case, the souls of the abusive men) that exerts such influence, even complete control, over the women's souls.

Women with needy, hurting, angry souls are just as liable to use soul power to control people around them as men are. For obvious reasons, there are not many women who physically abuse men to control them, although they may abuse other women or children. Women are capable, however, of affecting extremely strong soulish manipulation and control through non-physical means of mental and emotional coercion—guilt, fear, threats, soul-induced physical ailments (see Chapter 4, Healing).

Co-dependency is a term that has been severely overused in the past few years, but it is quite descriptive. The term was originally used to describe women whose lives were so intertwined with their alcoholic mates' lives that the women were considered to be indirectly (co-)dependent upon the alcohol as well. Nearly all classic "co-dependent" relationships involve soul-ties formed in an attempt to get unmet needs met. Both persons are seeking to get something from the relationship, regardless of how unhealthy or self-destructive it may be for them. The neediest people in these relationships often accept terrible trade-offs for what they blindly hope to get in return.

The Soul and Grief

It is within the soul that grief is experienced. Remember (see Chapter 3) that there is no such thing as a spirit of grief. If someone had a soul-tie with a person who dies, how strong that soul-tie was and how unwilling the remaining person is to let go of it, will determine the length of the grieving. I do not believe we need to go through long periods of grieving. The biblical Jewish custom of grieving the death of a loved one called for a period of several days of intense grieving with all family members and friends. Then those closest to the family would spend additional days with the grieving family members. After a designated period of time, everyone was supposed to get up and go on with their lives.

I believe God will extend all grace to empower us to acknowledge our loss, grieve for a period of time, and then surrender the loss to Him. That doesn't mean we should never think of the person again, with love and somewhat bittersweet memories, for it is natural to do so. However, the prior existence of soul-ties will allow excessive grief to continue on and on. While these residual ties can be severed, those in extended grief may not want to do so. These ties are the last remaining link they have to the ones now gone. These individuals become rooted in, even seeing themselves as defined by, "their grief." The soul-ties need to be loosed, detaching the remaining person's soul's power from the grief. Then God's Spirit can pour healing and peace into the soul of the bereaved one. This happened with David.

David had a son born to him of Bathsheba, and for certain reasons, God struck the child with illness. This is one of those scriptural passages (2 Sam. 12:14-23) that can bring forth some very interesting interpretations about what God will or won't do. David had sinned and God struck his son with a severe illness. David pleaded with God for the child, fasting and spending his nights on his face on the ground. Even though the elders of his household tried to get him to get up and eat, he steadfastly refused. In spite of all of David's fasting and protestations of faith, hope, and belief in a merciful God, the child died on the seventh day.

When David noticed his servants whispering among themselves on the seventh day, he asked, "Is the child dead?" They admitted this was so, fearful that he would do something desperate. But David got up, washed up, and dressed up—then he went into the house of the Lord and worshiped Him. David acknowledged his loss, rose up, and looked up to God and <u>released his grief</u>. David said unto his servants, *"Now that he is dead, why should I fast? Can I bring him back again? I will go to him, but he will not return to me"* (2 Sam. 12:23, NIV).

David desperately wanted God to spare his little son, but God does not always give us the answer we want. God is usually doing something beyond our present level of spiritual comprehension in those times that we just don't understand. David accepted his loss, knowing that no amount of grieving and pain of soul could bring his son back to him. He had to go on with his life until such time as he could go and be with his son in the Father's house.

Grieving Over Other Losses

Our grief is not always for the death of a loved one, sometimes it is for the death of our own unfulfilled expectations. Consider the relationship of the prophet Samuel and King Saul. I believe Samuel may have been very fond of Saul, having great expectations of his kingly potential; but I think the old prophet also knew things were probably not going to go well for this handsome young king. I can't help but think that Samuel threw himself into pouring everything he had into Saul in hopes that the Lord would value Saul more highly.

Saul served as king and a mighty warrior until we read (in 1 Samuel 15) that he disobeyed the word of the Lord, which had been given to him by Samuel. Because of this, the Lord told Samuel He was rejecting Saul as king. Samuel pleaded with God all night long before he finally went and told Saul he had been rejected. In 1 Samuel 15:34, we read that until the day of his death, Samuel did not go to see Saul again. Samuel was grieving over the unfulfilled expectations he had for the young king. But God had other things for Samuel to do, so He pulled him up short in his grieving. In 1 Samuel 16:1 (NIV), God said to Samuel, *"How long will you mourn for Saul, since I have rejected him as king over Israel? Fill your horn with oil and be on your way."* Or, paraphrased according to Liberty, "Your grieving isn't going to change anything, Samuel. Get on with your life!"

Have you ever poured yourself into a person, a relationship, a job, a project, a home, that you begged

God to bless—only to see God reject it? Unless you can sever the ties of your soul to that rejected "thing," you will waste a valuable portion of your life grieving over your unfulfilled and unrealized expectations. Some people will wear themselves out trying to make something work that God has rejected. Let go of what God says to let go of. Check your life and cut loose that unfulfilled expectation that you may still be grieving over, perhaps an unrealized dream for yourself or a grown child. Stop mourning over things that aren't the way you want them to be or that haven't turned out the way you wanted.

God says to pick up your anointing oil, and go where He is telling you to go. Get on with your life.

Soul-Ties Between Man and Wife

The love in a perfect union in marriage before God must come from the spirits of a man and a woman. Love that comes out of godly, spiritual unity never grows bored or disappointed or cold when time passes and circumstances change. Love based in spiritual unity continues to see the gift in the other person when the gift wrapping begins to fray and wrinkle. The soul and the body express marital love, too, but the spiritual union between the husband and wife is the only thing that can be counted on never to change.

A soul-tie between a husband and wife comes from a mutual agreement that the other partner is first in line for the meeting of all needs, whether reasonable or otherwise. There are certain needs in wounded souls that no human being can ever meet. A meeting of some needs will certainly be accomplished in a marriage, for each partner is a gift to the other partner. But ties between the souls of the two partners cause a man and a woman to look to each other for assurance, healing, support, sustenance, answers, and guidance <u>before</u> they look to God. When one partner's dependency upon the other partner is excessively out of balance, it may seem flattering at first. But eventually this intense neediness begins to drain the partner who is always expected to meet the needs of the other one.

It is an issue of an unfulfilled soul in a man or woman that prompts the words, "I don't love you anymore." Or, "I can't stand you anymore, and I want you out of my life." These words come from an <u>unsurrendered soul's</u> <u>bitterness and resentment that its expectations and needs</u> <u>have not been fulfilled and met.</u>

Training-Wheel Prayer
for Breaking Soul Ties

Lord, I have been looking to another human being to fix the need and the pain inside of me. I have not made right choices and kept my relationship with this person in proper perspective. I want to be free from any emotional, intellectual, or self-willed ties I've let form, and I repent for allowing this to happen. Forgive me for having sought satisfaction and fulfillment from anyone other than you.

I now loose, cut, and sever any and all soul-ties I have willingly or ignorantly entered into. I reject these soul-ties and every soulish satisfaction they have provided for me. I loose them, reject them, renouncing them and every wrong agreement I have ever come into that birthed those soul-ties in the first place.

I bind myself to the truth of your love, care, faithfulness, mercy, and grace. Your grace is sufficient

171

for all my needs, hurts, and issues. I am choosing to bring my needs and vulnerabilities to you alone. I will no longer let fear overcome me when I feel defenseless and vulnerable. Instead, I will remember that this means I am in a place where my soul's walls and defense systems are down. I choose now to realign my thinking and confess that this is not a bad place to be. It is a good place to meet you—there on top of the fallen defenses and tumbled walls.

I will quickly call out to you to come as deep into my soul as you can, touching every dark spot with your grace and mercy. This vulnerability can surely be used as an open door to your grace, God, no matter how quickly my soul might try to reestablish its protective bars over it. I will not hesitate to run through this doorway towards you, for if I am not sure of what finally tumbled the defense systems I've been loosing, then I'm not sure how long they might stay down. There will come a time when they are completely gone, when my soul surrenders totally to you; but for now, I will continue to loose them until they can no longer be reactivated.

I've tried too long and too unsuccessfully to get my own soulish, human expectations fulfilled. Increase my awareness of the fallibility of my unsurrendered soul's expectations. Increase my awareness of old patterns of behavior I need to loose. Increase my awareness of the wrong thinking I need to loose and reject. Increase my awareness that I can trust you with everything I let you get close to. Help me to recognize every high thing I've allowed my soul to put up between me and you, and I WILL PULL THEM ALL DOWN. In Jesus' name, Amen.

8

Now, Just Do It!

Jesus said, *"I tell you the truth, <u>anyone who has</u> <u>faith in me</u> will do what I have been doing. He will do even greater things than these, because I am going to the Father"* (John 14:12, NIV).

Christians are meant to be walking on water, stilling storms, raising the dead, opening blind eyes, and more! The word "faith" (KJV, "believeth") as used here means believing "with conviction full of joyful trust, with faith <u>to give one's self up to Jesus</u>" *(Thayer's Greek-English Lexicon).* I believe this kind of faith/belief only knows how to serve the Captain of our faith in one way—with <u>complete abandon</u>! This kind of faith unerringly "knows that it knows" anything is possible with Him.

Jesus gave us the keys of the Kingdom (Matt. 16:19) to "put off" every preconceived idea, half-truth, wrong belief, hidden agenda, fear, stronghold, and mind-set within our unsurrendered souls that keeps us from believing we can do exactly what He says we can do. <u>Our job</u> is to take these Kingdom keys and use them to bring our bodies, souls, and spirits into perfect alignment with God's will in order to see it fulfilled.

173

In the first chapter, I referred to "seeing" a picture of myself in what seemed to be a gun barrel. I believe that God was giving a glimpse of our potential when we are working <u>with</u> Him: He has control of the trigger which "drops the hammer," and we are like the cartridges or bullets ready and waiting to be propelled from the chamber. We're the project<u>iles,</u> He is the One who does the propell<u>ing.</u> I cannot help but think of the humor of an eager-beaver bullet trying to propel or "throw" itself out of the gun barrel towards some target.

On second thought, it's not that funny after all. I've "been there" and "done that" myself!

Spiritual Reality or Soulish Role-Playing?

For years, far too many Christians have been trying to get their "act" together in a completely backwards mode. Ephesians 4:22-24 (AMP), says in part: "[First] *Strip yourselves of your former nature—put off and discard your old unrenewed self—which characterized your previous manner of life* . . . . [Then] *be constantly renewed in the spirit of your mind—having a fresh mental and spiritual attitude; and put on the new nature (the regenerate self) created in God's image* . . . ."

When we are unsure of how to first strip off and discard our old natures to be able to "put on" the new nature, we try instead to project a new-nature "persona" through an act of our wills. Regardless of a believer's good intentions for presenting a witness for Christ, such an ongoing "role" must be maintained. A genuine "fresh mental and spiritual attitude" is not a role; it is a reality that requires no rehearsing, no props, no script. It is a state of pure "being."

We will never successfully rehab our old natures to assume a spiritual role that can then be integrated into our new creatures' spiritual state of being. We must strip, put off, and discard the old and <u>become</u> new. This can be done once and for all. Using the keys of the Kingdom, as you are learning in these pages, will not only open the exit door for the old nature to vacate its stronghold in your life—the anointing of the Holy Ghost will grease the doorway to make sure your old nature slips out into oblivion with a relatively minor fuss!

Let's Get It Right

Our God is a very practical God, being neither fickle about nor wasteful of the life experiences <u>we insist</u> upon accumulating. He would rather lead us into more spiritually productive experiences, I'm sure—but He will use whatever we insist upon dragging home with us. After I had "brought home" so many wrong experiences that I thought I was going to expire, I heard one minister say she had told God she wanted to go home to heaven right now. He said to her, *"Are you kidding? I'm not spending eternity with you the way you are now!"* I'm sure He feels exactly the same way about me.

Everything I've been through <u>is</u> being turned into exactly what God wants me to take into eternity for far greater purposes than I've ever dreamed of here. My spirit looks into eternity and glories in this truth by faith. My soul doesn't have any such long-range goals, and it hates change! I frequently have to bat it around with the Word of God and say, *"Get down and shut up, soul! I'm being trained! I'm being strengthened and made holy and pure so I can work for my Father throughout eternity! I bind myself—body, soul, and spirit—to the will and purposes of God; and I loose any wrong patterns of thinking, wrong beliefs, wrong ideas that you've tried to hang onto.*

175

"Soul, you and I are making a change for the better! I'm going to come out on the other side of these fiery trials here on earth like fine gold, purified until I'm as translucent as the golden streets of heaven (see Rev. 21:21). *Then Jesus Christ will be clearly seen through every area of my life. Yahoo!"*

Three things have to happen before you will ever force your soul to change. First, you have to be thoroughly disgusted with where you are. If you're not and you attempt to change just because you're told you should, when you get a few miles out and the pressure starts coming down and the heat starts rising up, you're going to be in deep trouble. You will look back and decide that where you "were" really wasn't that bad after all! You will almost always turn back in defeat.

Second, you have to believe that there must be something better than what you have.

Third, you must believe that there is a means of your getting to it. Do you want to change? One of the very first things to do is change the way you've been praying, not only for yourself, but for others, too.

Reality Checks on Your Prayers

How are you praying for those who have used and abused you? Are you praying so purely for them that you can ask God to bless them right now with a double portion of everything you're still waiting for?

How are you praying for your straying children and family members? Are you praying for God to use you in any way He wants, no matter what the cost to you, in order to bring them back to himself?

How are you praying for that spiteful, back-stabbing person you work with? Are you asking God to shower

His blessings, goodness, and grace upon him/her through your every word and deed? In spite of his/her concerted efforts to harass you?

How are you praying for your pastor who you think isn't dynamic and spiritual enough? Are you asking God to pour blessing and revelation into him/her? Are you binding yourself and your whole church membership to an attitude of a total support until God's will for him/her is fully manifested? No matter how long that may take?

How are you praying about the fact that the church leadership appointed someone else to the ministry position you wanted so much? Are you asking God to anoint the chosen one so he or she will be so successful that many will benefit and He will be glorified?

I have prayed the binding and loosing prayers for myself for most of the past eleven years in order to strip away the personal self-interests in my soul. I don't have my wings yet, but I have stopped most of my projecting, requesting, and expecting answers to come according to my ideas of what is best. I have stopped giving God special instructions on how the prayers should be answered. It is really quite presumptious of any of us to think that we know how the chips should fall in any matter.

All we know and understand, as if looking through a glass darkly, are the immutable attributes of God's character and the guidelines of His Word. (See 1 Cor. 13:12, KJV.) We do not understand His ways of working out the daily details of our lives or the lives of those we are praying for, at least not until the answers have already come. His ways are not our ways and His thoughts are not our thoughts. (See Isa. 55:8.) When we're all caught up in struggling with why God isn't doing what we want, when we want, how we want, where we want it done, God probably isn't doing much of anything for us at all.

177

Except, perhaps, keeping us breathing until we get tired of fussing and give up.

The Shortest Distance to Victory

The shortest distance between the two points of <u>frustration and freedom</u> goes straight through the middle of our own souls! The shortest distance between the two points of <u>anger and peace</u> goes straight through the middle of our own souls! The shortest distance between the two points of <u>self-vengeance and forgiveness</u> goes straight through the middle of our own souls! Finally realizing this has helped me redeem a very large portion of the time I have left here on earth. I believe I have given up years of productivity, both secular and spiritual, because of the wasted time I spent reacting to people, things, circumstances, situations, and words. Now I work at maintaining a "reaction-free" life, always trying to ask myself these questions if something bugs me:

1) Why did that upset me?
2) How come there is still a hot spot inside of me
that made that barb like a heat-seeking missile?
3) Why haven't I been able to let God neutralize
that old wound yet?

I try to remember to focus on my vulnerability to the barb rather than focusing on the barb-thrower. I mentally "red flag" the now-revealed hot spot in my soul, asking Jesus to show me what I have built up or laid down that is blocking His grace and mercy from this area. We cannot hold our shields of faith steady and straight when we're also having to hold multiple layers of self-protection and self-control in place over unhealed hurts and unmet needs that we are afraid to trust Jesus with. In Galatians 5:2 (AMP), Paul says this to all Christians, *". . . If you distrust Him, you can gain nothing from Him. "* That's a scary thought for the control freaks who trust only themselves, isn't it?

Stop Pretending Everything Is Just Fine

Let us go back to the Scripture I quake before whenever I'm not sure I can walk the walk as well as I talk the talk: *"Do not be deceived and deluded and misled; God will not allow Himself to be sneered at— scorned, disdained or mocked [by mere pretensions or professions, or His precepts being set aside]. —He inevitably deludes himself who attempts to delude God. For whatever a man sows, that and that only is what he will reap"* (Gal. 6:7, AMP). This is speaking of pretending and professing something that isn't, in one of three possible ways: First, you choose to let your soul convince you that you really are acting on God's precepts, when you're not. Second, you hope blindly for "the best," while you try to convince others that you are obeying God's precepts. Third, you pretend and profess that you can't act on them, and that God knows and accepts this because of everything that has happened to you. None of these pretensions or false professions are acceptable to God.

You spiritually fulfill God's precepts and principles by focusing your belief in three ways, already having done whatever practical things you know to do (i.e., praying, avoiding known temptations, reading God's Word, etc.):

1) Let your **spirit** affirm and rejoice in what God has said He will do for those He loves. Speak words

of praise from your spirit, sing them out loud, rejoice in them quietly, or exult in them at the top of your lungs.

2) Make your **soul** concentrate on and rehearse how faithful God is. Do not allow it to dwell on the details of your circumstances or how impossible they look.

3) Make your **body** conform to your belief in the goodness of God. Put a smile on your face, walk with a spring in your step, stop acting depressed, cheerfully fulfill your responsibilities, get busy helping others, etc.

This is synergy of faith! The word "synergy" means "all of the individual parts of something working together in unity and harmony, the end result exceeding the sum of the individual efforts." When God is finally allowed to complete the perfect, divine alignment of our tripartite being, the ensuing synergistic action of our bodies, souls, and spirits will produce miraculous results greatly exceeding anything all three of them could do on their own! The key word here is "cooperation," every part of your being working in unity with every other part and with God.

Therefore, it is not helpful to your spirit when it bravely takes a stand of faith in the face of all negatives odds, and:

- Your mind is filled with doubt.
- Your mouth is speaking fear.
- Your lower lip is quivering.
- Your face is bleak.
- Your eyes are baggy from crying.
- Your knees are weakly wobbling.
- Your hands are flapping limply in every direction!

When your soul is fearful or unhappy, it will do anything it can to try to prevent a <u>unified expression of faith</u> that declares God is in control. Every believer has fallen into this trap, and recognizing it is the first step to avoiding it in the future. *The Amplified Bible* defines righteousness as *"conformity to the divine will in <u>thought</u>, <u>purpose</u> and <u>action</u>"* (Rom. 6:18). This is an excellent description of the believer's <u>soul</u>, <u>spirit</u>, and <u>body</u> being in alignment with His plans and purposes.

To think, look, and act peaceful and joyful, regardless of what tough situation is crowding in upon you, <u>is not</u> self-denial. It <u>is not</u> just making a "positive confession" as the ceiling is coming down on your head. It <u>is</u> a believer synergistically thinking by faith, speaking by faith, and walking by faith—faith being *"the substance of things hoped for, the evidence of things not* [yet] *seen"* (Heb. 11:1, KJV). Go ahead, put a smile on your face and act happy. It is just plain weird to watch puckered-up, pickle-puss Christians trying to convince the world how happy they are.

God Wouldn't—Would He?

I have failed several of God's assignments over the years because I believed what I wanted to believe. I also believed that I knew "exactly" what God did and did not want me to experience as a child of the King. For instance, I remember some particularly noisy, partying neighbors of mine back in the early eighties. I tried everything I could think of to pray them out of my "nice" neighborhood. I bound the devil and cast out "demons of partying, alcohol, drugs, loud stereos," etc. I, and other neighbors, even called the police from time to time. But nothing was ever resolved. I was miserable and I certainly had no peace or joy.

I was trying to "BEND" my neighbors' wills to <u>my will</u>, which just wanted them to disappear. Having to get up at 6:00 o'clock every morning, I felt perfectly logical, reasonable, and justified in praying for these pests to go away! Do you remember what a personal stronghold is? The logic, reasoning, and justification we use to protect our personal beliefs, right or wrong. I "knew" I was right to believe that it was God's will for me to get a good night's sleep so I could be a good witness at my secular job, therefore, these neighbors were full of the devil. Or so I was convinced!

Near the end of 1986 (after eighteen long, frustrating months), I began to get the message that what I was doing wasn't working. Well, duh! I went back to the new concepts God was giving to me about binding and loosing. I began to bind my raucous neighbors to <u>God's will and purposes</u>, while loosing the enemy's influence off of them. I bound them to the goodness of the Holy Spirit and the mind of Christ, loosing wrong beliefs and ideas from their souls. I prayed they would get saved, that God would help me to love them. In less than a month, they moved. Actually, they *fled!*

They never did let me witness to them, and they didn't get saved before they moved. But I bound them to God's will and purposes for their lives. Matthew 16:19 tells me that when I did that in California, it was done in heaven, too. I believe that God has followed them, perhaps even parked them right next to another praying Christian—one whom I hope gets down to the business of <u>praying right prayers</u> sooner than I did.

Praying Right Prayers

I've heard so many believers complain about

unbelieving neighbors, unsaved relatives, and heathen co-workers they have to be around. The complaint I've heard the most is from believers who want to leave their secular jobs because they just <u>know</u> "God doesn't want them" to have to listen to the language and jokes of the non-Christians where they work. I don't think God wants any such thing!

If all of the Christians in the Body of Christ only worked at home or with other Christians, who would witness to the non-Christian workers? Who would pray for them when they lost a loved one or received a bad report from a doctor? Who would they turn to when they needed hope and solutions to hard things they were having to walk through? Who would show them that Jesus loved them even in the midst of their bad language and dirty jokes?

On the other side, who would push the ease-seeking Christians to grow beyond their own comfort zones? The person they hardly know but sit next to in the pews on Sunday? I think not. Who in this world best exposes self-righteous and soulish Christians' lack of love, convicting them to change? Their best friends? Not very often. No, it's those terrible non-Christians (who seem to always be pressing, rejecting, criticizing, and mocking "us" good Christians) who can really push believers' buttons and ultimately make them face themselves.

What if the unbelievers were to say out loud what I believe many of them are probably thinking: "Hey, Christian! Show me that I'm wrong and you're right. Your T-shirts, posters, and cute little 'Jesus coffee-cups' haven't shown me a thing! Prove to me that your God could love me, that He could really change my life! You won't talk to me about God on your own, so I'm pushing you to tell me what I don't know how else to find out."

Christian, even if your soul is only in the beginning stages of being surrendered to and receiving grace from God, surely you can stretch yourself to hear these unspoken words.

When a believer is only interested in getting away from the unsaved, the non-believers know it. They are well aware of the things that soulish Christians say about them. "It's just so-o-o-o hard at my job every day with all of the worldliness, the evil spirits, darkness, and sin. I pray all the time that God will get me out of that pit!" A faithful and true, surrendered and available servant of God would <u>never</u> leave others starving in a pit while he went off to dine at the Father's table!

I really cringe when I hear someone say, "Nobody at work likes me because I'm a Christian. The Holy Spirit in me just convicts them so-o-o-o much, they don't want anything to do with me. They won't even talk to me." Oh, hogwash! If the people who work with these Christians don't like them, it is probably because they are just plain obnoxious about their self-perceived superiority as "children" of God!

Jesus <u>never</u> sought to be with just believers so He didn't have to hear anything but "Christian" words. Jesus sought conversation with the woman who had been married five times and was now living with a man who was not her husband. Jesus protected and freed the woman who had been brought before Him as an adulteress. Jesus forgave and loved the disciple who hotly denied he ever knew Him. Jesus spoke with, ministered to, ate with, walked with, loved, and forgave the sins of betrayers, thieves, whores, unbelievers, tax collectors, street beggars, and others that so many of us find hard to love.

If Jesus cannot walk, touch, and talk with "hard to love" people today through the vessels of our bodies, how will they ever know that His love and His truth is available to them, too? If God is not able to change us enough to love them regardless of their rough edges, then how can they ever believe He can change them? It is true that the carnal mind and the closed spirit of the unbeliever cannot receive the things of the Spirit. But a carnal mind in pain or frozen by fear can recognize the love of Jesus when it is being extended through a surrendered human vessel.

When God places believers in certain jobs, these are <u>God-given assignments</u>. Every fellow-worker is a personal ministry project. If a believer is not free to witness out loud at work, nothing is accomplished for the Kingdom of God by complaining to others about how he can't speak one word about God or the Bible. The desired mode of operation at that point is to get into behind-the-scenes, binding and loosing prayer—the kind of prayer that always gets the issues right. We need to recognize when we have been commissioned as undercover agents for God. This is the believer's real job; the secular work is only a cover.

A Very "Now" Gospel

The beauty of the good news of the Gospel of Jesus Christ is that it doesn't tell you to get everything in line and behave yourself, and then in twenty years everything will work out all right. The gospel gives us a very "now" Jesus who meets us right where we are. He meets us right in the middle of all the mistakes we have made and are still making. He meets us right in the middle of all the things we have done that have caused other people pain, and all He says is this: *"Are you ready to let me begin the untangling and fixing of all of this?"*

185

I made some terrible mistakes in my life. I bought into the great "American dream," back in the early 1960's, believing it included a cottage in the suburbs, a perfect husband who would be a white knight in shining armor and make all the wrongs in my life right, 2.5 kids, a dog, a cat, and a station wagon. And we'd all live happily ever after! All I took into my half of this marriage was a huge collection of unmet needs and unbelievable expectations. I expected my white knight to bring unconditional love, adoration, and all the answers to my needs.

I didn't know anything about being a good wife, and my husband didn't know squat about being a white knight in shining armor. In fact, he had the nerve to think that I should be his princess, prepared to meet all of his unmet needs and expectations. What nerve! We both ended up feeling cheated and betrayed, and we either fought constantly or gave each other the silent treatment. While we were battling to force each other to meet our expectations, our three kids were getting more and more unmet needs, unhealed hurts, and unresolved issues in their souls. Our "American Dream" marriage ended in a sad divorce.

A couple of years later, I became a Christian. I accepted Jesus Christ as my Savior during a time of spiritual teaching that said there were certain things God *had* to do in response to a believer's steps of faith. If we did "this," God had to do "that." I sincerely thought that if I believed hard enough and quoted the Word loud enough, God had no choice but to do what seemed right. I didn't realize that I would play a major role in the process of His answering of my presumptuous prayers. Be careful about what you pray—you're probably *numero uno* on God's list of the steps that must be taken to bring the solution!

At Least God Showed Them Grace

Until approximately 1986, I did not know how to effectively pray for my children's freedom from the effects of the mistakes that their father and I made. Consequently, they were set up to overreact to their own unmet needs, unhealed hurts, and unresolved issues when they flamed out of control in adolescence in the late seventies and early eighties. This resulted in rebellion against their father, against me, and against God. I'm afraid God is the only one who dealt with their actions with grace.

At my lowest point of despair, concurrent with the highest point of the struggle with my children, God began to birth this message in me. And I finally began battling for them in the spiritual realm, withdrawing from battling with them in the natural realm. There was nothing I could do to erase the mistakes I had made with my children, any more than I could "erase" the mistakes my parents had made in my life, or the mistakes their parents had made in their lives.

I am now aware that whenever family members, who are all "guarding" their unmet needs, unhealed hurts, and unresolved issues, are put together under one roof—day after day after day—negative things are going to happen. The self-protective walls and strongholds they have built will become even more prickly and fierce unless someone knows how to start breaking them down to let God in. And those who are full of fear and pain will aggressively resist anyone, especially God, getting close enough to "get in."

After many tears and fears from mistakes I made with my own family members, I finally said, "God, I'm so sorry, but what do I do now?"

He said, *"Bind them to my will, and loose <u>the effects</u> of the mistakes you made in their lives."* You <u>can't loose the mistakes</u> you've made in any of the relationships with your family members. You made them, they did happen, they are facts of the past, and you cannot loose a fact. But you <u>can loose the ongoing effects and influences that have resulted from those facts</u>. When I began to do that, the whole structure of my family relationships began to change, and many healings were begun.

Training-Wheel Prayer for Family Members

I know I am to love my family with the love that springs from you, Lord. If I do not or cannot seem to love every single one of them, I have not entered into any real depth of relationship with you. There is no way I could not love them if I have made room for your love to fill me. Your love is alive and active, like your Word, and it does not sleep or hide. It is always gently pushing to flow out of any vessel you have filled. Lord, if love is not coming out of me and flowing towards even the most difficult members of my family, then I am in the greatest need myself.

I bind myself to your will, purposes, truth, mind, mercy, grace, and love. I loose every old shred of grave clothes from my life—the soulish irritation, frustration, resentment, jealousy, anger, hatred, unforgiven offenses, etc. I loose the velcro backing off my soul's desires for retribution—I rip it off and shatter its hold on me! I will no longer seek to settle scores with any family member!

Help me to become a vessel of love and understanding to those who have put down my faith and made fun of me. Help me to see that these put-downs are really cries from deep inside of them, pleading with me to prove that they are wrong about my trust in you. Help me to increase my prayers for the ones who are "crying" at me the loudest. Help me to change, so I can show them that God can change their lives—and the proof is me!

I bind my parents (and in-laws) to your will and purposes. I ask that you increase the faith and knowledge of Christ in the ones who know you. I bind all family members who do not have a personal relationship with you to your will and your truth. Please send angels, Christians, circumstances, and grace into the lives of those who once knew you, but have turned away to walk the paths of the world. I bind them to the paths you have ordained for them to walk in—straight back to you! I will no longer mourn and grieve over their fate, for I know you will move to bring them back into your family.

I bind my children to your will and purposes. Surround them with mercy and grace, even with hedges and thorns if they are trying to pursue the ways of the world. I know the sinful behaviors they are acting out are being manifested out of unmet needs, unhealed hurts, and unresolved issues in their lives. I loose the layers of self-protection that they have built up over these areas of vulnerability that they perceive as weaknesses. I ask that you pour your healing grace into their souls so that they will know you have healed them and made them whole.

I believe they are headed right to you, the God of the universe, the Author of their creation. I believe they are realizing right now that they have been created by your special design to fulfill awesome purposes and plans that will bring them great joy.

I ask for their salvation, Father, according to your will. For Jesus has told us in the written Word that it is not your wish that any should perish, but that all should come to know you. Lord, you want them saved—I want them saved—and I believe down in their deepest, most inner parts, they want to be saved. I believe in the mighty power of agreement in accordance with your will. I'm agreeing with you and with that smoldering spark in their spirits, no matter how small, that they will all be gloriously, wonderfully filled with faith and saved. I believe nothing can prevent this supernatural miracle from occurring in their lives! In Jesus' name, Amen.

Loosing Grave Clothes From Others

The Body of Christ has been taught for years that "you can't help someone who doesn't want help, you can't heal someone who doesn't want to be healed, you can't save someone who doesn't want to be saved, and you can't deliver someone who doesn't want to be delivered." I totally disagree! I didn't want to be helped, healed, saved, or delivered, either, when God began to draw others around me to show me His love.

You can loose negative things from another person. The story of Lazarus, a man who fell sick and died in the natural realm of life, gives you the spiritual parallel for doing it today. (See John 11.) Lazarus's family and friends came to a point where they decided there was no more use in praying, helping, or believing for healing because he was "dead." These were the same people who wrapped him in grave clothes and sealed him in the tomb.

Then his closest friend and loved one, Jesus Christ, came on the scene. Jesus made the people who had given up on Lazarus a part of the deliverance He was about to manifest. Jesus told the people who were standing around murmuring about the demise of Lazarus to roll the stone away from his tomb. Then He called out, *"Lazarus, come forth."* This is the only point in this particular scenario where Lazarus had to make any choices about what was happening—Lazarus had to choose whether or not he wanted to respond. Poor Lazarus was sort of "out of the loop" during the rest of the time. He was dead.

In those days, dead bodies were wrapped in grave clothes before burial, with a funeral napkin over their faces. When Jesus Christ called Lazarus to come forth out of that burial tomb, Lazarus <u>heard</u> His voice, and I believe he knew who was calling him. Bound in grave clothes, he probably struggled to blindly inch his way out of the tomb. He could not see anything because of the funeral napkin over his face. He only knew Jesus was out there somewhere, for he had heard His voice.

I can imagine him stumbling and halting in his bondage, unsure of what was restraining him, unsure of why he couldn't see Him who was calling him back into life. More than likely, he was also quite unsure of why there was no light to guide his steps. At that point, Jesus Christ told the people who had gathered to mourn Lazarus's death to now loose the grave clothes from him and set him free. The very people who had put the grave clothes on Lazarus and sealed him in darkness were now made a part of the miracle by loosing the grave clothes from him so he could walk into the light.

What are the grave clothes we are to loose from those who are bound up today? <u>Whatever is hindering their response to the voice of Him who is calling them</u>—word curses, wrong agreements, slander, wrong teachings, fears, doubts, wrong beliefs, unforgiveness, etc. They've heard His voice, be assured. They just don't understand why there seems to be so much stuff and darkness between them and Him. Much of that stuff, the grave clothes, comes from those who have decided these unsaved ones, these rebels and backsliders, are probably spiritually dead, gone, and hopeless. Grave clothes also come from "well-meaning" Christian relatives and friends who have exposed every detail of the lives of those who are bound and faltering—their failures, their sins, their secrets—in the name of sharing "prayer requests"!

We've done so much harm in the name of showing others that we're not in denial of our loved ones' problems. We've done so much harm in believing that we must be detail-specific when we want others to agree in prayer with us. One of the most incredible aspects of praying the binding and loosing prayers is that you do not have to figure out the details of another person's sin and bondage and then make decisions concerning how to pray about them. And you don't have to share private things better left unsaid in order to get someone else to agree with you.

You bind those who are in darkness to the attributes and characteristics of the Father, Son, and Holy Ghost: God's will, the truth, the mind of Christ, the control of the Holy Spirit, the Word. You loose strongholds, wrong patterns of thinking, wrong motives, deception, denial, and wrong agreements from them. You can stop trying to discover and deal with all the gory details. That is the Holy Spirit's job, anyway!

Grave clothes are hung every time you share the intimate details of your child's drug abuse, your cousin's homosexuality, your mate's infidelity, your boss's tax-cheating, or your friend's pornography problems. The Church should be the safest place in the world to bring your concern over such details, but it is not. These same details, once spoken into existence, can seem to take on a life of their own. Then, when prayers are answered for the lost one's salvation and restoration to the family of God, these returning lost sheep can find themselves faced with a nasty residue of the revealed history of their past actions.

In addition to fighting the devil and struggling with their unsurrendered souls that are slamming them with shame and feelings of guilt, they have to also overcome curiosity, legalistic watchfulness, and self-righteous judgments. Give them a break, please!

What Right Do We Have to Bind Others in Prayer Any Way?

What gives us the right to bind another person's will to God's will? Or another person's mind to the mind of Christ? I was surprised the first time I heard these questions, and at a loss as to how to prove how and why we could and should bind other people's wills to the will of God. I only knew such praying worked, and I felt it had to be the most sure thing God could want me to pray for others. As much as this reasoning satisfied me, I did not expect anyone else to accept the issue as forever settled. Maybe we can settle this once and for all now.

■ **Proverbs 24:11-12, KJV:** *"If thou forbear to deliver them that are drawn unto death, and those that are ready to be slain; if thou sayest, Behold, we knew it not; doth not he that pondereth the heart consider it? And he that keepeth thy soul, doth not he know it? And shall not he render to every man according to his works?"*

■ **Proverbs 24:11-12, AMP:** *"Deliver those who are drawn away to death, and those who totter to the slaughter hold back [from their doom]. If you [profess ignorance and] say, Behold, we did not know this, does not He Who weighs and ponders the hearts perceive and consider it? And He Who guards your life, does not He know it? And shall not He render to [you and] every man according to his works?"*

■ **Proverbs 24:11-12, NIV:** *"Rescue those being led away to death; hold back those staggering toward slaughter. If you say, 'But we knew nothing about this,' does not he who weighs the heart perceive it? Does not he who guards your life know it? Will he not repay each person according to what he has done?"*

■ **Proverbs 24:11-12,** *The Message: "Rescue the perishing; don't hesitate to step in and help. If you say, 'Hey, that's none of my business,' will that get you off the hook? Someone is watching you closely, you know—Someone not impressed with weak excuses."*

■ **Jude 23, KJV:** *"Others save with fear, <u>pulling</u> them out of the fire . . . ."*

■ **Jude 23, AMP:** *"<u>Strive</u> to save others . . . ."*

■ **Jude 23, NIV:** *"<u>Snatch</u> others from the fire . . . ."*

■ **Jude 23,** *The Message: "<u>Go after</u> those who take the wrong way . . . ."*

These verses are not speaking of people being drug into hell because of the devil. All who stand at the edge of his fire stand there as a result of wrong, free-will choices they have made in order to walk in paths of destruction. God will not violate or cross their free wills because of His own reasons, but God's Word is clearly telling me one thing: *I am to do nearly anything I can to stop them!*

Do not forbear to deliver them that are drawn unto death!

Those who totter to the slaughter, hold them back from their doom!

Rescue those being led away to death!

Hold back those staggering toward slaughter!

Rescue the perishing, don't hesitate to step in and help!

Pull them out of the fire!

Strive to save them!

Snatch them from the fire!

Go after them!

How are we to obey these commands and know we will not be found wanting in God's balance scales, clinging only to weak excuses? Should we stand stoically at the edge of the fire, holding protest signs and offering witnessing tracts? Should we give our testimony to them? Should we display our lives as a light that we hope they will follow? NO! Someone at the edge of the flames needs aggressive intervention, and a passive protest or gentle testimony may be too little, too late. We must do the most powerful thing we know how to do to obey God's Word and challenge their path. This is no time to worry about offending anyone!

Unfortunately, most of us still have unhealed areas in ourselves that pull back from possibly offending someone by confronting his spiritual state. If you haven't dealt with this, and some near you are in immediate danger, don't go home and try to first work through your issues of shyness or pride. Get down and get aggressive on your knees. Contrary to some opinions, getting on your knees to pray is not a "passive" position. You're never so righteously aggressive or spiritually tall in God's eyes as when you're on your knees, praying past any input of your unsurrendered soul. Begin to bind and loose for those lost lambs every chance you get. Do it in private. Do it in hiding. Do it in bed; do it under the bed. Just do it!

Great forcefulness is implied in these Scriptures, not only for what we are supposed to do, but also in the consequences of any lack of our obedience to this direct commandment. We're being closely watched to see if we are obeying this word from God. There won't be any excuses we're capable of coming up with that will be able to explain away a lack of our own accountability when God says, **"What did you do to prevent that lamb's death sentence?"**

Training-Wheel Prayer
for the Backslidden and
the Unsaved

In the name of Jesus Christ, I bind _____ to your will and purposes for his/her life. I bind _____'s mind to the mind of Christ that he/she will hear the very thoughts, intents, and purposes of His heart towards him/her. I bind _____'s feet to the paths you've ordained for him/her to walk in—paths leading right into your arms. I bind his/her hands to the special work you've ordained for him/her to accomplish in the Kingdom. I bind _____ to the work of the Cross in his/her life, for it is out of the crucifixion of self that your forgiveness, love, mercy, power, and authority will be able to flow through every area of his/her life.

I bind _____ to the truth of the goodness of the Gospel of Jesus Christ, to the truth of your Word. I loose all preconceived ideas he/she has about you, Lord. I loose all half-truths he/she has believed about you. I loose discouragement, deception, and denial from him/her. I loose the unforgiveness and its power that _____ has set up as a command post in his/her soul, fueled by the offenses he/she is holding against friends, family, and Christians. I loose the soulish arguments, human logic, and reasoning that _____ has used to justify not wanting to be around your people. I loose the lies the enemy has brought him/her into agreement with that have clouded his/her mind about your people.

I bind _____ to every word of Scripture that he/she has ever heard. Father, you have said that your Word will never return unto you void. The Word that I know he/she has heard in the past, the Word you sent forth to him/her for your purposes, I ask that you call it up from the bottom of his/her spirit and place it before him/her. Let it not leave his/her sight, no matter where he/she looks.

I bind _____ to the sweetness of your love, to the drawing and wooing of your Holy Spirit. I bind _____ into your care, and I loose the wrong thinking that has caused him/her to flee from being under the shadow of your wings. I bind him/her to the truth of your grace and your mercy. I loose guilt and fear from _____, wrong ideas that he/she has done too many sinful things, that he/she has gone too far to be accepted and forgiven by you. I bind him/her to an understanding of the concept of grace—your wonderful grace.

I bind _____ to recognizing the truth of the freedom and liberty of the truly surrendered and committed believer who knows he/she is loved by you and who knows how to love others with that same love. I bind him/her to the awesome truth of your great plans and purposes for his/her destiny. I loose all generational bondages, religious bondages, fleshly bondages, and soul-ties from him/her. Lord, in Jesus' name, I cut, sever, slash, and break the bondages of the world from him/her. I bind_____ to the truth of recognizing the depression, discouragement, and dishonesty that comes from believing the lies of his/her unsurrendered soul and the devil.

Move upon _____ by your Holy Spirit, Lord, and draw him/her to yourself. Lead Christians across his/her path who are similar enough to interest him/her, yet different enough to intrigue him/her. Cause angels to minister to him/her, getting his/her attention in supernatural ways. You are such a great and mighty God. I am so grateful that you desire to save all those who will give you even the smallest opening in their spirits. I believe that nearly every non-believer wants someone to prove that you are real. Let me be part of that proof to whomsoever you would bring my way. In Jesus' name, Amen.

9

Tying Up Loose Ends

In 1991, before *Shattering Your Strongholds* was published, I had a very uncomfortable confrontation with an extremely strong-willed Christian. We finally worked our way through most of it and I headed for home. As I was driving, anger came raging up out of the depths of my inner being. It so overwhelmed me that I pulled off the side of the road. Then I heard a smug voice whisper, "Try your little binding and loosing prayers on that!" Prior to 1985, I would have instantly started binding evil spirits and the works of Satan. But this rage was not a work of an evil spirit. It was a long-buried anger and sense of unresolved injustice over a similar confrontation I had experienced as a young person.

Because that buried anger had never been resolved, it just continued to fester within my soul like a simmering pressure cooker with its "stopper" stuck. I had no idea it was still inside of me, and I had never applied binding and loosing prayers to anything as "strong" as this. I was now face-to-face with the biggest question of my ministry and message: Would the binding and loosing principles work on the really big issues as well as the smaller ones? I was in a test that I had to complete, and I feared what the outcome might be.

I struggled to say in a very small voice, "*I bind my mind to the mind of Christ and I loose all of my wrong thought patterns, old beliefs, and attitudes that set off this reaction. Lord, you said whatever I would bind and loose on earth would be bound and loosed in heaven. I'm believing you to fulfill that promise now.*" The rage instantly dissipated, and I felt like a little tree after a tornado had just passed by. Then it hit again with increased force! I repeated my prayer with a little more conviction. Again the anger dissipated, only to return in a few moments with one final thrust of power. This time, I shouted the prayer out of the force of the faith welling up inside of me. The anger was finally gone.

My soul had been storing this sense of raging injustice for years with a hidden agenda—somehow, someday, someone would pay. The other person in this particular confrontation nearly did!

Many in the church world have been taught that evil spirits are responsible for out-of-control emotions and, therefore, binding the spirits will help free someone from a forceful emotion like rage. If I had bound an evil spirit and the rage had disappeared, I would have believed this happened in response to having bound the spirit. I would have believed that I had really outsmarted and defeated Satan (the surrogate enemy, in this case), hallelujah, glory to God! And, my soul would have just continued to simmer, biding its time, waiting for revenge. Believing I had just won the battle, I would have stayed ignorant of the real problem.

My unsurrendered soul was the real problem! Both Satan and your soul will back off anytime a disappearance of symptoms causes you to believe whatever charade either one happens to be currently running on you. Generally, your soul thinks it is the only player involved. Satan knows exactly where every player is on the board.

Binding and Loosing Naturally

Prayers of binding and loosing are now so automatic to me that when something going "thump-bump" in the night awakens me, I usually just raise my head and say: *"In the name of Jesus, whoever or whatever you are, I bind you to the will of God and I loose any fear from myself. Beat it."* Then I go back to sleep. If there is something I need to wake back up and do, I believe God will have an angel "thump-bump" me on the head. If one does, I'll do whatever he says. Selah!

A lot of things don't bother, unbalance, devastate, or trouble me like they used to, yet I'm still surprised when I see this actually manifested in my life. During the two weeks before I left on my final ministry trip of 1996, computers were blowing up, printers were gumming up mailing labels, newsletters needed to get out, outside production people were messing up my tapes and chart orders, and so on. Every action geared towards getting the newsletters, resources, and me in the mail and on the road seemed to be moving sideways or backwards.

I managed, through binding and loosing prayers, to inch ahead with a small amount of mental, emotional, and organizational victory. On the night before I was to fly out of state, I breathed a sigh of relief as I thought, "All I have to do now is get in bed, get up in the morning, and get on the plane." Then I turned around and did a backwards flip over the open door of my drop-front

201

dishwasher, landing on my head. Things swam around me a little bit while the only thought I could formulate was, "Well, I'll be!"

I finally crawled into the living room and got into my easy chair, feeling really "spaced out." I phoned a few people to ask them to pray for me, then I bound myself to God's will and purposes, to the paths He wanted me to travel in the next two weeks, and to His timing. I loosed any wrong beliefs or conventional wisdom that I was going to be in a lot of pain (everything my previous experiences with back and neck trauma and doctors was trying to flash into my mind!), slowly finished my packing and then went to bed.

During this two-week trip on the road, I was reminded of how God keeps bringing my own life further and further along in this message. When all was falling down around me (including me!) on this critical final night at home, I just kept binding myself to God's will and purposes, looking for His direction. I knew I was bound to God's will, and I wasn't going to step out or "fall" out of it. Furthermore, I wasn't going to let the devil push me out of it! It was a great trip, and I came home with the final understanding and unction to sit down and finish this book. Real victory always comes whenever we don't react to circumstances around us, but instead act on whatever He has said to do. Binding and loosing has made that possible for me.

Doing What God Has Said To do

None of us knows whether any wounded and bleeding lamb we meet is a desperate person in need of help, a hidden gem needing a gentle prying from its hiding place, or an opportunity God has set up to show you where your heart really is. In a meeting a few years ago, I noticed several very heavy women. I knew these women had suffered much—from Christians as well as non-Christians.

As I was preparing to minister to the first overweight lady in the prayer line after I finished preaching, I received a very direct word from the Holy Spirit: *"Pray for each one of these women like you were praying for Miss America."* He assured me that He had endowed each woman in that line with special qualities of mercy, compassion, hope, grace, beauty, tenderness of heart, sweetness of spirit, wisdom, and counsel. God then anointed my prayers beyond anything I could have drawn out of my own ministry experience. Each one of those women collapsed into my arms and soaked me with tears as I prayed, some having to be supported just to get back to their seats.

I knew they had rarely been ministered to without the inclusion of prayers that God would teach them new eating habits, show them how to understand nutrition, deliver them from overeating, supernaturally cause them to lose weight so <u>they could finally be used</u>, etc., etc., etc. These dear women responded in near-spiritual-breakdown when the Holy Spirit had me pray for immediate opportunities to be used of God, that they would speak words of faith with signs and wonders following, that God would give them divine appointments with people in high places.

I prayed they would be anointed to take healing and deliverance to many who had great <u>spiritual need</u>—ministers and church leaders, government leaders, and kings—not just those who <u>appeared to have the same struggles</u> they did. I thanked God for their beauty, their strength, their talents, their faith, and their ministry. I thanked Him for their wisdom, their understanding, and their value to His Kingdom.

Too often we are influenced in the natural by what we perceive to be visible "clues" of struggles in a life, or because we feel we have a "revelation" to pursue when something we say causes tears to fall. We need to come to a place where we do not depend upon any of our five natural senses for spiritual feedback. We really need to come out of the place where we aren't sure if God is moving unless the people we're praying for shake, cry, or fall down. Regardless of how spiritual we think we are, in our own wisdom we can miss the next Billy Graham or Kathryn Kuhlman that God is stirring up. We don't know who might be holding back a ministry of miracles, just waiting for someone to confirm that he or she has something valuable to give.

We must learn to minister as if we have sacks over our heads, oven mitts on our hands, plugs in our ears, and are treading water in a bottomless pool. Then we <u>will</u> minister according to God's leading alone, and the unrecognizable, not so obvious gems will be drawn out. Don't ever get to the point where you don't <u>need</u> to seek for and depend upon God's direction for every second of praying and ministry you do. If you hurt a lamb because you think you've "been there and done that already," both you and the lamb will pay for your arrogance and spiritual pride. Only the devil wins in this case.

Attitudes of the Unsurrendered Soul

The church world's emphasis on spiritual warring "against" Satan's purposes needs to be replaced with more emphasis on spiritual ministry "for" God's purposes. While many believe these two actions must work together, I believe they are to be more exclusive of each other than we've previously believed. In 1 Timothy 2:1-3, 7-9, *The Message,* Eugene Peterson translates Paul's original Greek writings in this way: *"The first thing I want you to do is pray. Pray every way you know how, for everyone you know. Pray especially for rulers and their governments to rule well so we can be quietly about our business of living simply, in humble contemplation. This is the way our Savior God wants us to live . . . . Since prayer is at the bottom of all this, what I want mostly is for men to pray—not shaking angry fists at enemies but raising holy hands to God. And I want women to get in there with the men in humility before God . . . ."*

Much of our current spiritual warfare, shaking angry fists at our enemies, is just posturing and pontificating, such as: "In the name of Jesus, Satan, I tell you that you cannot cross the bloodline here." Interestingly enough, many forget that while Satan may be stopped by the blood of Jesus Christ, the <u>rebellious attitudes</u> of our unsurrendered souls are neither behind nor under that bloodline. Unforgiveness is a perfect example of a rebellious attitude of the soul. Other attitudes of an unsurrendered soul include a desire for revenge, pride, grudges, self-righteousness, criticism, etc., but let's consider just one example for purposes of space.

Keep these points in your mind: <u>unforgiveness is not</u> an unhealed hurt, unmet need, or unresolved issue needing healing. <u>Unforgiveness is</u> a rebellious, disobedient attitude of the soul that needs to loosed along with the wrong beliefs and patterns of thinking that try to justify its existence.

Any outward expression of an attitude of an unsurrendered soul produces negative consequences, some sooner than others. For example, read Jesus' parable of the results of unforgiveness beginning at Matthew 18:23. After a great act of compassion and forgiveness on the part of the king toward a servant, the forgiven servant then refused to forgive another servant. The king was furious and rescinded his forgiveness to the first servant, delivering him over to the "tormentors" (vs. 34, KJV). In the original Greek, this word "tormentor" *(basanistes)* and its associated words *(basanizo, basanos)* generally mean "tormentor, torturer, inquisitor; one who brings pain, toil, and torment; one who harasses and distresses; one who tosses and vexes with grievous pains of body or mind" (*Strong's Greek Dictionary* correlation of 930, 928, and 931; also *Thayer's Greek-English Lexicon*).

These definitions fit evil spirits perfectly. (See Chapter 6 of *Shattering Your Strongholds* for further study of this topic). When the attitude of unforgiveness is not addressed and resolved by a believer, there is no bloodline in front of or behind that attitude to prevent evil spirits from tormenting, harassing, and vexing this disobedient and rebellious soul!

It is so much easier to impart forgiveness and grace to someone we know little about. Our unsurrendered souls are masters at rationalizing our choices to not extend the grace of forgiveness to those we know "too much" about. We judge what we know and feel justified in holding on to our unforgiveness, pain, and anger *"after the sun goes down,"* sometimes years of suns going down. This justification results in our giving room, opportunity, and a foothold in our lives to the devil (Eph. 4:26-27, AMP). The premise here is really quite incredible, if you think about it. Rather than simply obeying God and forgiving someone we have decided does not deserve our forgiveness, we would rather battle with satanic spirits. This helps Satan maneuver us into a spiritual survival mode.

Spiritual Survival Modes

As far as binding Satan, you can bind devils and demons if you want to, for the keys of the Kingdom apply to "whatsoever." But did you ever stop to think that for every evil spirit you bind, there are legions more ready and waiting to take its place? Did you really think Satan only had one available spirit to harass you? When you get the first one bound, who knows how many more spirits are "on call" to be next in line? This is the treadmill of a spiritual survival mode. It just goes on and on and on. The devil will <u>let you win</u> just as many pseudo-battles as it takes to keep you involved in that survival mode with him.

We simply are spending too much time today in spiritual warfare with our supposed external enemy, the devil—and too little time in spiritual dealings with our own carnal nature. One grand elder of spiritual teaching said on "The 700 Club" (in 1995) that he had changed his mind about retiring after God gave him a new revelation. God told him that for too long we've spent ourselves fighting the enemy without, while the real spiritual warfare should be fought against our enemy *within*. Yes! It is within our souls, our carnal nature, that we build our strongholds that open the doors to our external foe—thereby giving him the <u>only</u> means of access he has to our lives as believers.

If we would throw all of our spiritual battle time against the works of our unsurrendered souls, Satan would have no more doors of entrance to come after us. We would become lean and mean, armed and dangerous, ready to go out and give him a heart attack wherever he was attacking others who needed to hear the same truth. The believers who have surrendered their souls to God's purposes are the only believers who truly frighten our external, already-defeated enemy.

There are many believers who are sincerely frightened of the devil. Some have tied a knot and are trying to hang on. Some have retreated into their closets and won't come out until they hear the "trumpet" call that it's time to go home. Others just keep fighting and battling, hoping that somehow soon they will finally break through before it's too late. If these people keep getting beat up, taking hit after hit with no relief in sight, they finally begin to think about finding someplace to hide. Fear can be a hard position to come back from when it's time to move out for God.

So, am I walking all of this out in my own life today? Most of the time, eventually! Okay, I'll admit that I'm not always running around, frothing at the mouth, whipping the sword of the Word back and forth, ready to plunge it into the heart of the enemy's work. There are times when I feel quite underwhelmed by who I am and totally overwhelmed by everything else. There is little room for God in that equation, and I do get tempted to just hide under my bed. There just isn't any dignified way to do that, however, when you're six feet tall. So I head back into the binding and loosing prayers until I'm ready to hear whatever my Captain says next.

I bind myself to the truth and to an awareness of the

power of the blood of Jesus shed for me, and I bind my mind to His mind. I loose word curses, and I loose strongholds protecting the insidious little ideas and mindsets that have formed. I loose every device and hindrance the enemy may be trying to confuse me with. Then I head straight towards whichever Goliath is trying to scare me, using the sword of his own words to cut the head off the lies I briefly listened to.

No Fear?

There are genuinely fearful things in the world today—not the fear you vicariously experience when a hero or heroine is in grave danger in a suspense movie, when you're on a roller coaster ride, or when your little brother puts a snake in your underwear drawer. Let's consider the intense kind of fear that can cause you to freeze up, give up, even throw up.

Non-believers deal with many of their fears by chemically blotting them out (drugs, alcohol, tranquilizers, etc.), by self-empowerment seminars, by learning self-defense techniques, to name a few. They also flock to horror movies and read horror books which allow them to experience and laugh at fear in a surrogate setting. The basic problem with these two kinds of "no-fear" drills is that no one walks away from them impact-free when the last page has been read or the screen credits have rolled. The rampant evil in many of today's writings and films continues to impact their souls "behind the scenes."

During this decade, many T-shirts, car window decals, etc., appeared with the words "No Fear" written upon them. I never did really understand the intent of this, but one Christian T-shirt I later saw put things into perspective for me. It said: *Imagine this: The world has ended and you find yourself standing all alone before God at the great white throne of judgment. **STILL NO FEAR?***

Dismantling Fear

Fear can come from the vulnerable areas in our unsurrendered souls, from learned responses and reactions to traumatic situations, and from the harassment of evil spirits accessing the unsurrendered soul. Many of us have learned to try to create certain environments in which we feel relatively safe from fear. This requires us to avoid everything that frightens us, including people, situations, challenges, conversations, pictures, sounds, animals, emotional triggers, etc., that we know spark fear in us. Once we have all of our safe people and comfort zones drawn in round us, as well as all of the unsafe people and scary zones pushed out by our safety procedures, we can control a lot of our fear.

The success of this ongoing process is quite simple, if exhausting and maintenance-intensive: Avoid anyone, everyone, anything, and everything that could trigger any fear. This means of fear-control is practiced by both non-believers and believers with unsurrendered souls.

Believers who maintain a peaceful, serene demeanor in life through such intense self-control can be very convincing. Nothing seems to rattle or shake them—as long as their safety zone is intact. Many of these believers know how to control their fear only when they are around other people, requiring constant interaction with other believers. Things are different when there is no one to distract or comfort them and the fear closes in on them.

This believer is often plagued by feelings of hypocrisy, but the act must be played out lest others identify and thereby validate the existence of the fear.

There are some believers, however, who are completely deceived by their own self-constructed "safety net." These believers genuinely believe they have eliminated fear from their lives and their "peace" is real. When someone truly has the peace of God, no words or actions of others can shake that peace. Believers who wrap themselves in a soul-defended, soul-enforced "peace" zone will become upset if something is said that rattles that zone. They may be very firm about what you can and cannot talk about around them. These believers are in great denial of their fears, coping with their terror the only way they believe will work for them.

Pure prayers, filled with the truth of His Word and free of the influence of our unsurrendered souls, can dissolve all fear.

Training-Wheel Prayer for Breaking Fear

The Word says that you have not given us a spirit of fear, but of power, love, and a sound mind. Jesus, I declare in the power of your name, that I will not accept anything in my soul that you do not desire for me to have. I bind my body, soul, and spirit to your will, and I now affirm that you have all power and you love me—you will protect me.

I loose fear from myself, I loose all tormenting thought patterns, and I loose the strongholds that have opened the doors to allow the terror that comes in the night to trouble me. Holy Spirit, show me the doorways of access my strongholds have opened in my soul, and show me the sources of fear that I may be feeding on by watching wrong things on television or reading wrong things. I loose all desire from myself to want to look upon any images or words of darkness, wrong acts, and evil, supernatural forces.

Lord, I loose my layers of self-protection from the unresolved issues of my life. I confess that I am still not certain of where you were during those experiences when I have known extreme pain and panic. I open up these unresolved issues to you and ask you to neutralize my memories of them with your grace and your love. I do not need to know and understand everything about them now, for it is only my unsurrendered soul that wants answers. Reveal what you want now, and tell me the rest later in heaven. Heal the torn fabric of my trust, Lord, at the deepest level of my doubt and confusion over these issues. You are the only one who can!

I bind myself to the unchanging truth of your Word that I should fear not, for you are ever with me. I bind myself to the reality of your Word that says I should stand in faith when danger comes near—for the battle is not mine, but yours. I bind myself to your Word that says I am not to be dismayed or afraid of anything man, the devil, or the world would bring against me—for you are my shield, my truth, and my buckler. I bind myself to the reality of the truth that says I do not have to fear evil, even when it camps around me. I bind myself to the reality of the truth that your angels have already encamped around me, and they are stronger than anything the enemy or the world can throw against me.

Your Word says that a little sparrow shall not fall to the ground without you knowing it, and that I am of more value to you than your sparrows. Your Word says that I am like a lamb in your flock and that I can know and trust that it is your good pleasure to give me the Kingdom of your Son.

Help me, Holy Spirit, to think, to act, to walk, and to talk with full faith in the Father's love and protection. Let me not be a stumbling block to a world that sees no difference between so many Christians and themselves when it comes to fear. Let me show forth peace, faith, love, and grace, regardless of any storms swirling around me. Teach me, Lord, how to be a calming influence in every storm. Let me show the world that there is a difference when a Christian really knows you. In Jesus' name, Amen.

Faithless Fleeces

Have you ever prayed and prayed for something your soul desperately wanted, standing firm on your prayers for days, weeks, months, sometimes even years? In my early walk with God, I used to be afraid to let up on those kinds of prayers. I thought that God was just testing my ability to hold out for what I wanted and if I gave up, He'd think I wasn't serious after all. There were times when I didn't even still want what I was praying for, but I wouldn't give up! I was trying to set a precedent with God that I was a force to be reckoned with when I prayed. I sometimes think God kept me around during those early years just for comic relief!

God has reasons for refusing to answer your soulish prayers that are prayed amiss. I think He usually just ignores them (thank you, Jesus!). Satan does not ignore soulish prayers prayed amiss, however, and he is quite capable of answering some of them! He is also quite capable of seeing that you "get" fleeces confirmed that you think you're putting "before" God in your prayers. I don't rule out that God might still respond to the Gideon/ fleece method of praying, but it is definitely a "low-tech" approach to getting spiritual guidance. We have something Gideon didn't have—the Holy Spirit living inside of us to help us make decisions.

If you've prayed and prayed and haven't heard anything from God, chances are you've opened up a preset line of communication that is programmed to receive only the answer you want. If you have prayed amiss, God has no intention of using that line. And if you are convinced you know what the answer should be, you won't open up a surrendered line. Impasse! So, when you've waited as long as you think you can, deadlines have to be met, people have to be answered, etc., and you are way-too-spiritual to be openly rebellious—you may resort to the "fake fleece" gambit. This is the fleece that allows you to justify doing exactly what you wanted to do all along.

Almost all of our "fleeces" come from our souls. For example, imagine you prayed about charging an ocean cruise (that you can't afford) on your American Express card. You are frustrated that you have not been able to get a word back from God on this cruise, when you suddenly "think" of a fleece: the numbers 1195 (the cost of the cruise) on a green background (the exact shade your American Express card)! You don't verbalize this to a soul, "keeping it" just between you and God. That is how you protect the validity of a fleece, right?

So, within the next day or so, you go down a street you've never been down and you see an American Express green colored house with the numbers 1195 on it. <u>Well, that certainly has to be God, doesn't it</u>! So you charge the cruise on your American Express card and start buying swimsuits and sandals. Then you can't figure out why the cruise was a big disappointment, your job was cut when you got back, and American Express took your unpaid charge card away from you.

Didn't God give you a sure confirmation of the fleece you "thought" up, prayed about, and asked for Him to confirm? No. The devil knew you were planning to go down that street with the American Express green colored house (number 1195). He didn't read your mind—he saw you circle an address in your newspaper of a garage sale on the same street. Then he dropped the "fake fleece" idea in front of you. I've fallen for this myself! It is not hard to believe whatever you want to believe when you want something bad enough.

Taking a Walk With God

If you don't seem to hear anything on a given issue that isn't turning out the way you think it should, pray again and reaffirm that you are choosing to bind your will to God's will and **wait** for His direction. Don't try to come up with a fleece for God to respond to. He's very capable of showing you exactly what to do and when to do it, if you are capable of seeing and hearing. This divine form of communication works especially well when your soul's strongholds are being shattered and torn down on a regular basis.

The unsurrendered soul's attitude of "justified impatience" has caused many in the Body of Christ to land in all kinds of situations that abound with sticky tentacles and prickly ropes of bondage (also known as consequences). Loosing the natural consequences of a disobedient act will not always make them go away. Sometimes you have to go <u>through</u> the "school of consequences" to learn patience so you will avoid making wrong choices in the future. Loosing the wrong attitudes of your soul and binding yourself to His timing, however, will amazingly deactivate most if not all of the stress of any mandatory "consequence class" attendance as well as the time frames and deadlines of life.

I've had to do this in many stressful situations that I could not resolve, no matter how hard I tried. When I bound myself to God's timing, instead of man's timing and my timing, God worked things out. This doesn't give me license to be impetuous or lazy, for I am still accountable for the consequences of my choices. But when I've tried to bring my own actions and behaviors into line with godly principles and things are still seemingly messed up, I don't panic anymore. I let God do what He wants. I've learned that the hindrance to the answer that I think is best actually may be God setting up a roadblock because He has a better path for me to follow.

Imagine yourself and God setting out on the first day of your Christian walk on an almost parallel course of purpose—only one-tenth of a degree apart in your headings. You would "appear" to walk together for a time, but slowly that one-tenth of a degree difference would begin to angle your two paths further and further apart from each other. If we were left to our own paths, we would never end up at the same place as God on any given day—unless He did something to adjust our loopy sense of direction.

Most of us are off a lot more than one-tenth of a degree from God in our paths. This is why God has to keep adjusting and realigning us. God responds quickly to the right prayers of the believers who are open to His adjustments. I don't think He responds while He is waiting for us to stop our wanderings and hold steady for His adjustments. Still, God doesn't waste anything, not even our wandering mistakes. A good friend of mine always said that no matter what happens between the prayer and the answer, God is still always making saints of us.

Desperately Waiting For God

When you are desperately, frantically waiting on God for an answer, you must first come out of that place of feeling desperate and frantic. Don't say you can't, because you can. First, realize that God is never desperate or frantic over the resolution of a situation. He is far more interested in fulfilling His larger, eternal purposes than He is in reacting to your little temporal fit of panic. This does not mean that He doesn't care, but it does mean that He looks at things from a long-term perspective. Binding ourselves to God's timing helps us to relax, receive His peace, and hold steady for the blessing that always comes with cooperating with His timing.

While you're waiting for your answer, if you need something to occupy your time, concentrate on what God is doing in the lives of those around you. You may realize that He wants to display something so unbelievable through your situation that you'll hate yourself for the rest of earthly life if you miss out on it!

We have most of the New Testament today because Paul was completely surrendered to allowing God to fulfill His promise that Paul would go to Rome—however God saw fit to fulfill it (Acts 23:11). God "saw fit" to let Paul be put in prison where he would write the New Testament epistles which would impact time and eternity. What if Paul had gone to Rome in a high fit of righteous indignation, being consumed with his rights as he stormed the city like a little Tonka truck on steroids? How far do you think he would have gotten? But Paul prayed and obeyed. He looked for God's plans in whatever God put before him, wherever God put it before him. God's purposes for this period of Paul's life were gloriously fulfilled.

When you feel that you have prayed, obeyed, and stayed, as long as you can, the best course of action is still to hold steady and let God be God. Whenever you are in conflict about whether or not God really knows what you need the most, recognize that your spirit believes He does, but your soul does not. Your spirit must be in control of your belief systems to stop the conflict—a regenerated spirit and an unsurrendered soul will never be equally yoked in right beliefs.

Our conscious awareness of what we really believe about God resides in our minds. (Will He really do this for me? Does He really want me to be happy?) The non-believer only has the carnal mind of the soul with which to think on this, and the carnal mind is at enmity with God. Double-minded believers have the carnal mind of their souls in conflict with the mind of Christ in their spirits. These believers will vacillate from one extreme to the other, anxiously fretting first over the consequences of letting God take over and then fretting over the consequences of not letting God take over. A spiritually free believer has his mind bound to the mind of Christ, with Christ's peace and input empowering him to believe God cares and God is in control no matter what things look like in the natural. This person is just waiting for God's signal light to turn green.

Do not stop short in your faith. Do not tell God you can't wait for Him to bring you to the point where He can perform a miracle in your life.

10

Are You Ready for Your Future?

God will use every single believer who is diligently trying to dismantle his or her unsurrendered soul's control structure—in whatever way. It doesn't matter to Him who you are, where you've come from, what you've done, or even <u>what you are doing or not doing right now</u>! That's a shocker for some who feel they are hopeless failures. When you finally make a unified body, soul, and spirit, "no-holds-barred-burn-the-bridges-go-all-out-for-it" decision for God, He will respond with a mantle of greatness for you. He will immediately assign people and places and things to begin to move towards you. Divine appointments will begin to come into being, great hook-ups will begin to be made, and doors will begin to open that no man can shut.

There are no book-markers, no pew-sitters, no bench-warmers in this final age, so get out of any finite thinking you might still wading around in. You are living right now for a specific purpose. If you have not known how to step into fulfilling that path of purpose where God empowers you and supplies everything you need to fulfill His directives, then you simply haven't known where the doorway is. You now have the understanding you need to strip away all the layers of camouflage that have been hiding it from you.

We Will Impact Nations

We are not praying together enough today, especially for our own nation's leaders. We're much busier criticizing, dishonoring, and armchair-quarterbacking everything they are doing. We will never banish the darkness over this nation and our leaders by railing at them. We can only banish darkness by bringing forth the light! You already have everything you need to become armed and dangerous enough to shed light into the darkness on a truly grand scale.

Begin to pray in agreement with others to bind our leaders to the will and purposes of God, and then loose the wrong counsel of man, the power and effects of word curses, and strongholds from them. Especially loose the effects of word curses from them! Believers have been coming into terribly wrong agreements, praying soulish prayers, and speaking word curses over the leaders of America for years. Christians have never been worse about this than in these closing years of the twentieth century. Speaking such "spiritual" slander is very easy when the unsurrendered soul, instead of the spirit, is the seat of the Christian's "wisdom."

Some Christians can become quite sarcastic these days when someone says, "Let's pray for the president (or the Congress, or the Senate) to have wisdom and to hear from God." This is appalling in the face of the Scriptures that tell us that no authority is over us that God has not placed there, and that we are to pray for (not against!) all those in authority. How have Christians moved so far from the Word of God that says God will heal nations when His people pray? I believe part of this judgmental, critical decline of Christians' attitudes towards our leaders can be directly attributed to unsurrendered souls locking onto the tirades of the wildly popular, self-appointed, self-anointed media voices of the nineties.

Many times I have been asked what I think of the best-known "conservative" talk show host of this day, and I have carefully expressed a concern over the extremely negative words he constantly speaks about our nation's leaders. In response, I have been "branded" as a liberal more than once. I'm not a liberal, I'm not even a "card carrying" conservative, as conventional wisdom would define a conservative. I'm a Christian trying very hard to adhere to God's Word which says, *"If my people, which are called by my name, shall humble themselves and pray, and seek my face, and turn from their wicked ways, then will I hear from heaven, and will forgive their sin, and will heal their land"* (2 Chron. 7:14, KJV).

Please note that this verse does not say when the president, the abortionists, the pornographers, the thieves, the politicians, and the terrorists turn from their wicked ways and humble themselves, then God will heal our land. God has said He will heal our land when His people turn from their wicked ways and humble themselves to pray.

Someone recently asked me that old question that non-believers love to bring up: "How can a loving God let little children be abused every day? Why doesn't He stop that, if He's so full of love?" I've always struggled with answering that question, because no matter what I would say, I never knew if it would satisfy their honest need to know.

This time I heard myself reply, "That is not God's fault. It is the fault of the church world today. If every one of us who believes in Jesus Christ would humble ourselves, turn from <u>our</u> wicked ways and pray—without ceasing— God would stop the abuse and heal our land. We're the ones who are failing the hurting and dying of this nation." As His people, we should be praying everyday for the world's children, young people, unbelievers, gang members, policemen, government leaders, housewives, exotic dancers, athletes, church leaders, soldiers and veterans, plus everyone else.

How Should We Pray For Our Leaders?

Many Christians are not in agreement about how to pray for our national and world leaders. They will only agree on how horrible our government leaders are, and how our evil government is trying to close down or control our Christian schools, our churches, and Christian television. Once more, you do not defeat darkness by cursing it—you dispel darkness by turning on a light. If you are not able to share the light with world leaders—one-on-one, face-to-face—then pray for them to receive understanding and light however God wants to impart it. The following was birthed out of the type of prayers that my ministry's intercessors pray over our leaders nearly every week:

Breaking the Power Prayer
for Government Leaders

Jesus, your Word says that I am to obey, submit to, and pray for all those who are in authority over me. There are none in positions of authority and power that you have not allowed to be placed there—no president, king, governor, mayor, or any other leader has been elevated into power in this world without your knowledge and permission. Your Word clearly says that there is no authority except that which you have established.

The Word also clearly says that if I fight with, rebel against, disrespect, or gossip about those you have established in positions of authority, then I am rebelling against and fighting against what you have instituted. To do so means I will bring judgment upon myself.

Lord, forgive me for the words I have spoken about the leaders of my nation and the world. Help me to remember that I can only dispel darkness with light. I bind the president, senators, governors, mayors, (etc.) to your will and purposes, the truth, and the paths you have ordained for them to walk. I bind their minds to the mind of Christ. I bind their families to your will and purposes and to your constant care.

I loose wrong beliefs and ideas, wrong attitudes, and ungodly counsel from them and their staff members. I bind their ears to your voice, their mouths to the words you want spoken, and their eyes and hearts to the truth of your Word. I loose word curses, soul-ties, wrong agreements, political bondages, and generational bondages from them.

I pray that you will correct and chasten as necessary; strengthen, bless, heal, and encourage always; and send your Spirit to guide every leader in the whole world. I loose the power of all leaders' own unsurrendered souls that would interfere with godly decisions for their countries. I loose Satan's influence, hindrances, and devices from their thoughts, deeds, and actions.

225

*I bind the leaders of all of the countries of the world
to the paths you have ordained for them to walk in, and
to a full recognition of your sovereign leadership. I bind
Israel's leaders and people to your will and purposes.
Strengthen Israel and supply all that she needs to fulfill
her destiny in your plans and purposes for mankind. I
pray for the peace of Israel, Father, and I ask that you
guard Israel from terrorism, from disease, and from all
attempts of the enemy to harm the people there.*

*Lord, I bind your people to obedience to your Word.
I bind them to the truth of their need to humble themselves
before you, to repent and turn from their wicked ways,
and to seek your face. Lord, send forth ministers and
leaders with the message that <u>you have said you would
heal our land when the godly would do this</u>. Cause your
people to rightly judge their own responsibilities to this
nation and the world. In Jesus' name, Amen.*

Today's Church Leaders

The Body of Christ is growing rapidly in knowledge
in these last days, outrunning some of the church world's
leaders. Many ministers and spiritual teachers are trying
to keep up by preaching and teaching "beyond" their own
spiritual experience. We cannot minister life beyond the
level of our own experience with the Life-giver himself!
Nor can a heart be taught or trained beyond the point of
the unmet needs, unhealed hurts, and unresolved issues
within the soul.

This has lead to a returning to the prayer closet for
some leaders. It has resulted in legalism and bondage in
others who have feared their restless sheep may begin
seeking other flocks who appear to be feasting on latter-
rain grass. But blocking the gateways when the sheep

begin milling around is not the answer. Church leaders must press ahead of their flocks in godly living, seeking spiritual wisdom and a discernment of God's will for today. If the sheep are willing to follow, God knew they would. If not, God knew they wouldn't. Any leader who is trying to maintain soulish control of his or her flock will fail, for only the Spirit's anointing will settle the sheep in these final days.

We don't have to pray and read the Word from sunup to sundown while fasting for days to receive God's anointing. It is readily available. But we may have to study the Word for hours every day, fast for weeks, and pray for months in order to strip away our carnality, excuses, pride, reasoning, logic, and strongholds so the anointing can get out past the weasels of our souls! If we have to invest that much time in crucifying our flesh every time God gives us a sacred appointment, there will be a lot we will NOT be getting done! The time we spend in prayer, study of the Word, and fasting should be spent in order to deepen our relationship with God, rather than having to fight our way through our own soulishness.

We need to make room within ourselves for God's divine changes, letting Him move us out of our own limited understanding and resources into His. We can't expect Him to hand us the keys to the family car if we've never been willing to give up our scooters. We have to progress through the stages of our maturity His way. He's not going to change His plans or His timing, because they are best and right. Regardless of whatever visions and/or prophecies you've heard that some great leader had recently, no one knows exactly what God is beginning to do today. And I think we're all going to be quite surprised by who will be the first to actually know.

We need to loose all of the preconceived ideas and wrong beliefs we may have ever formed about how we can anticipate God's will and ways of doing things in these last days. This needs to be accomplished for Him to speak important facets of His deeper truths to us and for us to pray clearly and purely to Him.

Twelve-Step Program For a Progressive Prayer Life

This is a guaranteed program/methodology/formula for a progressive prayer life that will not fail! Write it down and make sure you don't lose it. Step 1: PRAY. Step 2: PRAY. Step 3: PRAY. Step 4: PRAY. Repeat first four steps two more times. If fear, doubt, worry, anger, apathy, unforgiveness, concern, anxiety, or stress reappear, repeat entire formula as many times as necessary.

I pray binding and loosing prayers for everyone that I intercede for in my family, my relationships, my church, my city, my country, etc. I even pray them for people I find in the newspaper and see on television. Every day I turn to the sports section of my local newspaper where the ads are located that feature the latest topless-bar dancers and strippers. I lay my hand on the faces in the ads and pray binding and loosing prayers over them, asking God to bathe them in mercy, grace, and love, drawing them to himself for healing. I pray binding and loosing prayers over people on the streets, people in parking lots, people in grocery stores, and elsewhere.

I occasionally have people tell me that this is not the only way to pray. They say, "What about the people who lived and died without ever knowing how to use binding and loosing prayers on their unsurrendered souls? How did they ever make it without your book? This is not the only way to pray, you know!"

Well, of course I know that. However, think about this: Imagine being locked inside of a fortified, multi-walled, brick building all by yourself. No lights, no cell phones, no beepers, no homing pigeons, no windows, and you want out. There are various things you can do to try to break out, dig out, or crawl out through ventilation ducts—some of them will eventually get you out. But what is the fastest, easiest, surest way of getting out? Use a master key to open the doors!

This is the beauty of the promise of Matthew 16:19, *"I will give unto thee the keys of the kingdom of heaven; and whatsoever thou shalt bind on earth shall be bound in heaven; and whatsoever thou shalt loose on earth shall be loosed in heaven"* (KJV). These master keys—binding and loosing—not only open the doors of human, soulish, and demonic bondage to let you out of your self-prison, they also open the doors that let you into a greater fullness of His Kingdom right here on earth! You can even use these master keys to open doors for others, as well.

Cooperating With God's Will For Others

Almost every single "challenge" I get on the right to bind and loose for other people comes from former occultists who are now Christians. I'm sure this is because they have a heightened super-sensitivity to anything that could be construed as mind control. I believe their intense concern over being controlled often clouds their ability to see certain truths. Satan's counterfeit use of binding and loosing principles has preceded their understanding of God's purposes for the same principles.

I will confess that for many years I really struggled with trying to figure out why we were supposed to pray, getting others to pray as well, before God would seem to be willing to act in certain circumstances. I don't know if I ever admitted this to anyone before, but here goes: Prior to my salvation experience, I would get really angry at people who told me they were going to call their prayer chain to get as many people as possible to pray for a need in my family. I believed God wouldn't do anything until He got the level of attention He wanted. Once again, I reiterate that I am only here today by the sheer grace in God's character—I have no idea how else I ever escaped becoming a "crispy critter" over and over.

I may have been the only new/carnal Christian who ever tussled with that, but it was very real to me. Finally, about fifteen years ago, I just reached a point where I stopped questioning why He did things the way He did. But I still didn't completely understand why God would frequently not act until people prayed.

Dr. Alfred Marshall's KJV-NIV Interlinear Bible gives the following interpretation of the original Greek meaning of Matthew 16:19: "I will give thee the keys of the kingdom of the heavens, and whatever thou bindest on the earth shall be[,] *having been* bound in the heavens, and whatever thou loosest on the earth shall be[,] *having been* loosed in the heavens."(the inclusion of [,] by author for clarification—in line with J.B. Phillips' explanation below). The foreword to Dr. Marshall's work is written by J.B. Phillips (a well-known translator of Scripture) who says in part:

"I am glad, for example, to see that Dr. Marshall has not missed the peculiar Greek construction in Matthew 16:19 where Jesus tells Peter that 'what he binds on earth' will be 'what has been bound' in Heaven. There is a world of difference between guaranteeing celestial endorsement of the Apostle's actions and promising that his actions guided by the Holy Spirit will be in accordance with the Heavenly pattern."

This is not the first time I have found a translation of Matthew 16:19 similar to Dr. Alfred Marshall's and J.B. Phillips's explanations here. But this understanding is the clearest I have seen. I believe this amplified understanding is telling the Body of Christ this:

Using the keys of the Kingdom, binding and loosing prayers, is our way of cooperating with and participating in the earthly, natural manifestation of these words of the Lord's Prayer, *"Thy will be done on earth as it is* [already determined] *in heaven"* (author's inclusion of phrase [already determined]). Is it possible that Scripture does not record Jesus Christ actually using keys of binding and loosing in prayer because He didn't need them? He already knew how to cooperate with and participate in anything the Father wanted done. We're the ones who don't! We're the ones who need all the help we can get in learning how to fully cooperate with Him!

Is it not mind-boggling that God, for some infinitely incredible reason, wants His people to be a key part of the earthly manifestation of things already settled in heaven? Whew! This is <u>not</u> a restating of any doctrine, movement, or "ism" that implies or promises that we can control and move the hands of God by our prayers, or that we can claim certain things and outcomes by speaking faith-filled words. So many believers want shortcuts that will bypass God's will and time frames. I want to state J.B. Phillips' writing once again, paraphrasing it slightly for clarification:

> "There is a world of difference between guaranteed celestial endorsement of *our words and prayers* and (Jesus) promising that *our* actions guided by the Holy Spirit will be <u>in</u> <u>accordance with</u> the heavenly pattern."

All prayers from hearts that are hungry for answers are heard by God, but I believe some prayers are more in direct alignment with an earthly manifestation of God's will than others. I choose to pray the way I believe the Scriptures tell us Jesus provided so we could learn how to overcome our old natures and fully cooperate with God's will—<u>God's will only</u>—not my will, nor the will of any other earthly believer.

"Letting Go And Letting God" Be God

There are innumerable creative ways in which God wants to involve us in a manifestation of His will here on earth, particularly with the seemingly unreachable people of the world. But He can't use us if we're always going to be stressed out by His stretching work in our lives. When we're filled with fear, insecurity, and touchiness, He knows we will react soulishly to anything pressuring us into extending the stakes of our tents beyond familiar ground. He knows that raw, open wounds, unresolved doubts, and fears within our souls will hinder us from fulfilling the really big assignments He's waiting to give us.

Until we take our self-protective layers off the vulnerable areas of our own wounded souls, He can't heal our wounds, resolve our doubts, and neutralize our fear and pain. When we prevent Him from doing that, we limit our usefulness to Him. Nearly every Christian wants to be useful in the work of the Kingdom in some way, from the most timid of lambs to the strongest of the lion-hearted rams. Lion-hearted believers do not always have an edge in the areas of usefulness.

Cooperating with God's final healing processes isn't going to be the easiest for those who are the strongest, the bravest, and the most determined to succeed. It will be the easiest for those who understand the two most important attributes of their character—attributes which the devil has no weapons against—**obedience and submission**. A believer's complete obedience and submission to God's will in situations that make no sense to the human mind—that are not logical or rational according to conventional wisdom—will open up the flood gates of His supernatural, miracle-working power.

Every person who holds an end-time position in God's army must learn how to move out of their own efforts and striving and into the freedom that comes with moving in the anointing of God's Holy Spirit. These "end-time positions" include being in the "open" in a five-fold ministry, seemingly "behind the scenes" while raising children in the home, or in an "undercover" position in secular employment. In other words, each one of us, every single Christian in the world, has come to a point in time when it is critical to cut every soulish comfort zone we've ever depended upon—the familiar, the comfortable, the usual, and the expected.

We are all going to be launched out beyond our own familiar territory into new areas where any remaining soulish areas within any of us—the need to feel safe, to be understood, to be approved, to feel important, etc.,—will be sorely tried and strongly pressured. God will attempt to move us all into a new dimension far beyond our human foibles and fears. This will be position of solid knowing, way beyond "blind" faith, that all things really are working together in every situation.

Every Christian's expectations of these final last days is too finite. Time will become like a clock with no hands. It will be passing, but it will have little relationship to the assignments we will be undertaking. All believers with deep desires to leave their former ways behind and embrace the next wave of God's purpose need not fear being passed by. God will not pass one tiny church by, reject one discouraged minister who thinks he or she has failed, nor overlook one quiet lamb who wants to be used. The call to come will be extended to all who want to be called, as well as many who never dreamed they could be called. The only prerequisite to this call to all believers will be obedience and submission to His will and His divine assignments.

God has a divine destiny for every believer alive today, whether they've been in the spirit for years, or in the soulish realm for even more years. He's holding out His hand to lead His people out of religion as usual. I've only sensed a tiny peek into what will be coming, just as others have sensed minute glimpses of God's stirring of the spirit world. Sometimes I awake in the night and realize another unsurrendered area in my soul is coming apart as I "see" shattered pieces and tiny shards flying in every direction, as if an iceberg had just exploded. I awake in the night with detailed answers to nagging little problems I've had no idea for solving. I awake in the night and sense small areas of anxiety and concern melting away. There is a metamorphosis occurring in my innermost, spiritual being, which is slowly radiating out into the reality of my natural life.

One woefully inadequate way I can try to explain is to relate an experience I went through in 1995, when I was surprised to realize that I had changed and grown beyond myself yet again. I had moved on with God and didn't even realize it until I took a two-hundred mile trip with Him.

The Anniversary Party

One morning in July of 1995, I was preparing to drive to another town to hostess a retirement party for my seventy-five year old mother combined with a fifty-seventh wedding anniversary party for both my parents. I prayed and bound myself to God's will, purposes, and timing as I always do before getting ready for any trip; then I got in the shower, washed my hair, and dried and styled it. It was a genuine "good hair day," one of those days that are priceless and precious to women when they occur! I wanted to lock in my "look," so I searched for my bottle of hair spray.

My traveling assistant had efficiently already loaded my bags into the car, so my toiletries were all outside. Muttering about "efficiency-nuts," I dug around under my bathroom sink until I found an old bottle of hair spray.

After several big squirts, I wrinkled my nose at the unusual smell, wondering, "Does hair spray go 'bad'?" But, bad hair spray seemed better than no hair spray at that point, so I sprayed on even more. The obvious lesson here is that you should never store Ortho Home and Garden Bug Spray (or any other weird thing) in an old hair spray bottle under the sink!

Reeking of bug spray, I got back into the shower and reshampooed my hair several times, washing off all my makeup, to emerge still smelling slightly like a cockroach that "got away." I had run out of time to redo my hair and makeup, so I just jumped in the car with dripping hair and a shiny nose and started up the freeway. Faithful to my calling and my message, I prayed again and bound my used car (nearly 140,000 miles old)— named "Shadow" because it was the *shadow of the perfect car yet to come*—to God's will, purposes, and timing. But a short distance up the road, "Shadow" began to knock, overheat, and slow down. Concerned that the air conditioner running on high was adding to the problem (it was 102 degrees outside), I turned it off and put all the windows down. The hot air rushing in the windows was like a giant hair dryer! My hair began to blossom as my perm began to blow.

Determined to press on, I kept binding my car and myself to God's will and purposes and timing, convinced He would fix everything. Shadow kept going slower and slower until, some thirty miles from my destination, I was "racing" up the freeway's edge at fifteen miles-per-hour. I stopped to call my parents and told them to go on and start the party without me. I had rented a little ballroom, ordered dinner for some fifty people, and hired a 40's music deejay and a video man, so I felt things would be okay until I got there.

My son, Rusty, drove out to meet me and determined that I had no transmission fluid and Shadow's "transaxle" was fried! By pouring container after container of transmission fluid into the transaxle because the fluid kept mysteriously "disappearing" every few miles, we finally made it to the party. By now, of course, I looked like a demented dandelion, with my hair puffed all out, and I was covered with grease. I had been crawling around under Shadow's hood "helping" my son (like I knew what I was doing!).

With only one-and-a-half hours left before we had to vacate the "ballroom," I made my entrance into this special party which was filled with old family friends and extended family members. This was not how I imagined I would return into the lives of some of these people I had not seen for nearly thirty years. I had hoped that someday the "mighty woman of God" would come back into her old home town with a police escort, a parade, and a big, white limousine. Then these people, who had known me for decades, would be amazed at how the ugly duckling had become a beautiful, godly princess.

But I walked into this little ballroom looking worse than they had ever seen me, dripping perspiration, streaked with grease, with a red face and puff-ball hair. I briefly reassured them all was well and dashed to the bathroom to try to pull myself together. I yanked open my travel bag (which had been on the car's floor right above the overheating transaxle) to find that the intense heat had caused a large jar of face cream to explode. My change of clothes, jewelry, curling irons, makeup brushes, etc., were all swimming in hot, white goop. Looking heavenward, I whispered, "God, we are going to talk about this later." Then I just closed my bag and went out to party! There really seemed to be nothing else to do.

I became the social butterfly of the night—flitting from table to table as I had one of the best times I've ever had at such a gathering. I didn't understand a thing about what was going on or why I was having such a good time, but I figured God and I would take that up at home. As everyone began to depart some time later, family members and old friends alike came up to me one by one to say good-bye. They all expressed great amazement as they remarked, "I can't believe how you're taking this. I just don't know how you've seemed to have so much fun. You've **really changed** from the way you used to be. Unbelievable!"

Later that night, I settled into my bed and said, "Okay, God (He had not yet said a word all that day), let's talk. I got up this morning and bound myself to your will and purposes. I bound my feet to the paths you wanted me to walk. I just don't understand this. I bound myself to your will!"

He said, *"I know you did."*

"God, I bound myself to your timing!"

He said, *"I know you did."*

"God, I bound that car to your will and purposes!"

He said a little louder, *"I know you did."*

I finally began to detect a pattern here, so I quit talking. As I did, God began to speak. *"You have finally reached a point in our relationship where I can use you in ways I never could before. You would not have been flexible in my hands before; instead, you would have*

238

thrashed around, become very angry, and ruined everyone's evening. That is how most of your family and oldest friends still remember you.

"Many of the people there tonight would never listen to you preach to them of my power to change their lives. They would never open my Word and read how the blessings of my imparted grace and joy could change their lives. But tonight, they saw living proof of my power to change a life they believed was unchangeable—yours.

"They will remember this 'living sermon' far longer than any other message you could have preached from a pulpit. You and your car were exactly in the middle of my will. I sent you on assignment today <u>to reach the unreachable</u>. You succeeded, even though my purposes were completely out of the realm of your understanding. Well, done, daughter."

Tears began to slide down my face as I realized how once again an awesome God had mysteriously moved in His infinite wisdom in the midst of something that was beyond the realm of any of my logic and reasoning. This was truly a case of my having to let go of all of my plans and purposes and let God pick up the pieces, or so it seemed. But God had every detail planned out perfectly and, for once, I didn't mess His plans up! That is the most amazing part to me, that I was able to be used in ways outside of my natural understanding and <u>I didn't mess it up</u>. Hallelujah!

I have finally broken through old patterns of thinking, old beliefs that I have to control all the details, old attitudes of how important it is to show others that I can make things happen, that I know exactly what God will and won't do. Others recognized that change in me and were astounded at a God who could do that. Some are finally asking questions I wondered if I'd ever hear. (P.S. God gave me a gorgeous new luxury car right after that—a car that I would have never dared ask Him for. There are no burdens to the blessings He sends when we obey. Oh, yes, this car's name is Blessing!)

Reaching the Unreachable

Nothing is ever going to change this last generation until they see real, visible, tangible, life-changes in us— God's people. Too many Christians today talk wonderful testimonies, but there are many old negative patterns of thinking and reacting to circumstances that are still operating in their daily lives. These same Christians complain and worry about the government, the economy, their pastors, their bosses, their spouses, their children, their lives. The world watches and listens and wonders why anyone would want to give up the few crutches it has access to—alcohol, sex, drugs, escapism—to have to "bite the bullet" while living a life that seems no less painful, less stressful, or better than theirs.

How many people are still waiting to know of a God who does things they have never dreamed of, all because we have pre-formed mind-sets about the acceptable limits of how God wants to use us? How much do we miss receiving from our heavenly Father every day, all because we're so busy trying to figure everything out ourselves? How many tough things, hard spots, and unfathomable situations do we stumble and struggle through our way, or what we think to be the "Christian way," rather than surrendering to God's way?

Ephesians 2:10 (AMP) says this: *"For we are God's [own] handiwork (His workmanship), recreated in Christ*

Jesus [born anew] <u>that we may do those good works</u>
<u>*which God predestined (planned beforehand) for us,*</u>
<u>*(taking paths which He prepared ahead of time) that we*</u>
<u>*should walk in them—living the good life which He*</u>
<u>*prearranged and made ready for us to live.*</u> " What a God!

Givers of Grace

I think we're all going to be very surprised when
we get to heaven and hear what God asks us. I don't
think He's going to bring up every failure and slip we
ever made. I believe His questions will have just one
theme: What did you do with the deposit of His grace
that He placed within you? Did you minister the healing
power of His grace to others who were in pain? Did you
take His grace to those who didn't know anything about
it? What did you do with His grace that He placed within
you? He meant for it to be disbursed to <u>everyone</u> you
come into contact with.

We have a tendency to be very free with His grace
when we are around people we know little about. It is
much harder to extend grace to those we know all about—
their every wrinkle, wart, and rotten deed. But Jesus
poured all grace on us, and He certainly knew every awful
thing there was to know about us. We must stop deciding
who is or isn't good enough for our forgiveness, our
unmerited favor, and our dispensation of God's grace.
His grace is so sufficient, so good, ever so much more
available and accessible than we realize.

Isaiah 55:1 (AMP) tells us, *"Wait and listen, every*
one who is thirsty! Come to the waters; and he who has
no money, come, buy and eat! Yes, come, buy priceless
[spiritual] wine and milk without money and without

241

price [simply for the self-surrender that accepts the blessing]. " I had nothing good to give to God twenty-five years ago, but I surrendered as much of me as I knew how. He washed me, saved me, and blessed me anyway. He did this even though He knew I was probably going to cause all kinds of scuffles in His Church for the first thirteen years of my Christian walk. God saw something in my heart during that whole time that told Him **what I couldn't get my mouth to say or my actions to show**, "Lord, I want to do right. I want to serve you. I want to be useful to others. Help me become your servant, God, because I don't know how."

Reality-Checks for a Servant's Heart

I have a couple of little reality-checks that I occasionally run on my soul to see what might still be buried under old layers of self-control and self-rights. One of them is to put myself into potentially-humbling positions in order to see how my soul's level of dying-to-self is registering. This is one reading you can really deceive yourself about unless you force your soul into a confrontation about its Oscar-potential "acting" ability. Whenever I do this, my soul charges around to dig up all the embarrassing memories it can find of previous humiliations and painful times of being really humbled, hoping to scare me out of my reality-checking. This is actually a big mistake on its part, for then I begin loosing the self-protective layers from these old memories so God can neutralize them.

Some reality-checks are as small as seeing if I can let statements about my previous "positions" in life slide by without updating the "statement makers" that I am now a published author, ordained minister, traveling Bible teacher—blah, blah, blah. For example, I was a church secretary and a freelance typist in the late seventies. I occasionally run into people twenty years later who want to know if I'm still "working for the church" and typing for people. When I'm doing pretty well on the dying-to-self register, I respond, "No, I'm working and typing just for God now." If I'm not doing so well, I usually run my mini-resume for them. Whenever I do that, no matter how humble I try to sound, I always walk away wishing I'd developed lockjaw fifteen minutes before I ran into them.

God keeps blessing me with little training sessions that are helping me become "more dead" in this area. One man I had never met (he was related to someone from my past areas of employment) read my first book, got very excited about it, and called me to order several copies. After we finished having a delightful conversation, he said as he hung up, "I can't believe that God would give such an important revelation as this to a church secretary!"

I chirped, "Isn't God good?" and thanked Jesus that I had passed another reality check.

Shortly after that, a pastor of a very large church in another city called the ministry office and asked to speak to <u>Ms. Savard</u> about <u>the book</u> named *Shattering Your Strongholds*. Right away, I knew we were going somewhere I didn't really want to go. I identified myself and he said, "<u>Ms. Savard</u>, just what is your point of integration for the body, soul, and spirit?" (I thought to myself, 'Say what?') After several more pointed questions, I realized he was trying to prove to himself whether or not I really comprehended what was in the book, and I think he was even trying to determine if I had really written the book.

He finally paused, sighed, and told me he would like to order several more books for his pastoral staff. He was really having a hard time! He probably couldn't believe that God would give this revelation to me, either, for his parting remark was: "It's been very interesting talking to you, Ms. Savard. I can almost forgive you for being a woman."

I bit my tongue, swallowed the blood, and chirped, "Isn't God good?"

This would not have been the case just ten years ago. I would have reacted in such indignation that I would have surely burned every bridge in sight and then found myself all alone on an peak of "self-indignant-self-righteous-self-vindication" with no way to ever get down from it. I would have created an impassable, impossible canyon between myself and this man, his ministry, and his church, "proving" to him that he had been right all along about women in ministry. I am so grateful that God has been able to get into the deeper areas of my soul!

Lessons often come in bunches (remember how I said God loves threes?) and shortly thereafter, a church in Southern California, where I had previously preached, invited me to come and present my books and tapes at a conference they were hosting. I was sure they would probably call me back and ask me to teach in one of the sessions or to give a workshop, but they never did. The word was: Just come and be our guest. That may be what they thought, but just before I left, I felt the Holy Spirit was telling me that He had another agenda in mind.

I flew into the airport, rented a car, and drove to my hotel, where I went to the pastor's room and told her the Holy Spirit had said I was to be a servant to her during the conference. A pastor of over ten years, she wisely said, "Well, if that is what God wants you to do, then let's find something for you to do to serve me. You can press my clothes."

Now, some people might have said to me, "Oh, that's just so sweet of you! But you don't have to be my servant; God will bless you for just offering." She didn't say anything like that, because she didn't want to get in God's way. So, as the different conference speakers drifted in and out of her room, I gritted my teeth, smiled sweetly, and pressed her clothes with as much grace as I could muster. When I was about to go back to my room, she said, "You can drive me to the conference in my car. I'll be ready in about forty minutes."

Whoops! I still have one teensy-weensy, little-bitty stronghold in that area. I want my own car, whenever possible, even if it is not practical. I replied sweetly, "Oh, no, I just rented a nice new Oldsmobile. You can ride with me."

She looked a little funny as she said, "I have all my things in my car, and it would really be too much trouble to transfer it. You can drive me in my car. Besides, you don't know the way to the church from here."

"Then I'll follow you," I called over my shoulder and hurried out of her room and down the hall. The minute I closed the door to my own room, however, the Holy Ghost was all over me about how a servant should do whatever she was asked to do. I countered that I would pray for this pastor, I would hold her jacket, I would carry her Bible, I would get her whatever she might need, and so on—but I didn't want to drive her car and leave mine behind. Of course, I finally had to give in to Him. In more than a bit of a snit, I called her room and said (ungraciously, I'm afraid), "Oh, all right.

245

I'll drive you in your car. I don't want to—but God says I have to!"

Instead of being intimidated by my unservant-like attitude, she replied, "Good. He told me that you would." Believe it or not, I had to bite my tongue to keep from accusing her and God of talking about me behind my back. My soul was really acting up! Throughout the conference, I did whatever she asked (none of which was unreasonable), while no one else asked me to do another thing—no signing autographs, speaking, opening in prayer, leading worship, etc. Talk about a reality-check!

I learned that I can have a wonderful servant's attitude when I'm under the anointing, teaching, and ministering to people. But, when I'm not under the anointing and I'm not preaching and praying for people, I still have "a ways" to go. I have a lot more to learn about being another person's servant, but I'm seriously working on getting a certificate in this area.

Pull the Plug on Your Pride

If you are lacking in a servant's attitude, go back to binding yourself to God's will and purposes again, loosing wrong ideas and beliefs about how spiritually important you are. Also loose the layers over the unmet needs in your life that cause you to believe you are being taken for granted, belittled, ignored, or "dissed"—whatever particular lie your soul tells you. Let God get to your unmet needs and meet them. This will effectively take them out of the realm of being manipulated by your soul.

How does your soul manipulate an unmet need in your life? If one of your unmet needs came into being because no one ever affirmed you during a critical point of development in your life, the drive coming out of your need for approval will push you into continually seeking praise and appreciation from others. You will thrive only when you are being singled out and commended for being who you are, which is at cross purposes with the role of servanthood. As long as your soul can manipulate the unmet need, it can quite effectively thwart any attempts you make to become a servant of God <u>in truth</u>, while it "acts" out a charmingly false role of humility and graciousness.

God is faithful to reveal the hidden purposes of your soul in the secret of your own spirit if you let Him. It is not His desire to bring forth such things publicly, but you can't just act humble when you're the center of attention. If your humility isn't real, sooner or later, God will see that you are exposed as a hypocrite! He will expose the hidden agendas of your soul when you insist upon trying to meet your own needs. Something that motivates me to be constantly loosing any layers and strongholds and self-denial from myself is a fear of God having to expose a buried sin in my life before a huge crowd of people who are all looking at me!

"O God! Melt me, mold me, shape me, and crush me even. Whatever is necessary! Don't let me build up self-protective devices that allow me to walk around denying my need to change when you know I need to. Do anything, say anything, ask me to do anything, whatever you want to get hidden deception out of me and your truth into me—just please don't let me take any hidden thing with me when I go out in front of hundreds of people. Ple-e-e-e-ase!"

247

True Humility

Years ago I worked as the administrative assistant to the head pastor of a large church, and I was responsible for the lodging arrangements for those we brought in to minister. One well-known minister who travels around the world was supposed to come and speak on a big holiday weekend. His assistant called me two days before the man was to fly in with his family, wanting to verify that all the arrangements had been finalized. I assured him that we had reserved a nice room at a motel right across the street from us, a brand new Motel 8 where our speakers seemed very comfortable.

The assistant seemed shocked, replying that he would call me right back. A few minutes later, he did— with the news that something had come up and the minister would not be able to fulfill his engagement with us after all. Thank you, good-bye. CLICK!

A few months later, Mark Buntain flew in from India to be the main speaker for our annual missionary conference. Mark Buntain and his wife worked for years with the orphans of Calcutta, running a huge orphanage. He wrote a wonderful book about his missionary work there that I wept over, feeling his love and compassion for those little Indian children. With some concern and trepidation, at the pastor's orders, I booked Brother Buntain into the now only-nearly-new Motel 8. I nervously called him after he had arrived and asked if everything was all right, or did he want to move.

"Oh, no," he cried. "This room is just a blessing. Why, I've just been going around the whole room, from corner to corner, thanking God for His kindness and His goodness to me. There are so many in India who are sleeping in the streets. Here I have this wonderful soft bed, a view of the swimming pool, and a big, white tile shower. Why, I even have my very own little coffee pot to make coffee any time I want to! It's just wonderful. Thank you so much for everything."

I may not always remember the name of Brother Buntain's book, I may have even forgotten his message from that missionary convention. But I will never forget the genuine delight this world-famous, mighty man of God had in a Motel 8 room with a soft bed, a white tiled shower, and a personal little coffee pot! He was very important around the world and certainly in my eyes, but he wasn't important at all in his own eyes. I'll never forget the lesson he taught me that day.

Brother Buntain, now home with the Lord, had already allowed God to heal all of his unhealed hurts, meet all of his own unmet needs, and resolve all of his unresolved issues. He was completely unconcerned about and free of any personal expectations of anything or anyone. All of his concern was for others. If I ever learn to be one-tenth as humble and appreciative of God's blessings in every corner of any room as that precious man was, I'll be happy. If an "image" remains when I go to be with Jesus, I'd like to hope that it could be a little like I remember Mark Buntain.

Training-Wheel Prayer
for Ministry

Lord, I am so grateful that you have saved me, are healing and teaching me how to walk in the Spirit, and that you are going to use me in the manner for which you created me. I bind my body, soul, and spirit to your will and purposes for my life. I bind my mind to the mind of Christ, I bind my will to your will, and I bind my emotions to the control of the Holy Spirit.

I bind my feet to the paths you have ordained for me to walk: to the mountains and to the valleys, to the continents and to the islands, to the dark alley ways and to the bright streets. I loose all preconceived ideas and patterns of thinking that I have ever had about "my" ministry, or about other's ministries that I have either coveted or not understood. I surrender all my dreams, visions, plans, and preparations to your will. I loose any wrong attitudes, motives, or desires that my soul is holding on to. I loose all of the offenses I've ever held on to, all of the unforgiveness, all of the hurt feelings from when I felt I was being overlooked.

Lord, I want my one desire for ministry to be that your will is always able to be accomplished in and prospered through my life. I know that I need to be a clean, empty vessel in order for that to happen. I want to be emptied out of all of the things of this world, of my old nature, of man's ways and plans, of preconceived ideas, of religious and doctrinal mind-sets I have allowed to form in my soul. I don't want to leak out any ungodly mixture into my ministry, only a flowing forth of the anointing of your Holy Spirit.

Let the fruit of your Holy Spirit fill me as I loose and strip away the old grave clothes of my soul. I want to show forth the unique characteristics you have formed in me, but I don't want any attitude to frame them except love, joy, peace, patience, kindness, goodness, faithfulness, gentleness, and self-control. Your Word says that those who belong to Christ will be able to manifest these fruits of the Spirit, because they have crucified their sinful nature with its old passions and desires. Lord, I loose the control and power of my old nature—my unsurrendered soul—and I loose all wrong desires and passions from my unsurrendered will.

Let me minister your love to those I come in contact with every day. Let me remember that love never fails, it is always patient and kind. It does not envy, it does not boast, nor is it proud. Love is never rude or self-seeking, not easily angered. Lord, above all else, teach me to remember that <u>*love keeps no record of wrongs and offenses.*</u> *I loose, crucify, sever, and strip away my soul's desire to keep files and accounts on others who have rubbed me the wrong way.*

Show me how to desire only to protect others in their struggles, instead of wanting to expose their faults. I know your Holy Spirit in me can always protect me, so I can offer non-judgmental trust to all. Let me remember to always keep giving out your love to the world, showing them how you have changed my life.

Father, keep turning up the heat of your refining fire to get all dross out of me. I want to be as pure as the finest gold that is nearly transparent. Only then will others see just Jesus in every act of ministry that I manifest. I bind myself to the paths you have ordained for me to walk, to your timing, as well as to the paths, places, doors, divine appointments, and assignments you have purposed for me. In Jesus' name, Amen.

Workings of the Unsurrendered Soul
Full-Color Laminated Charts With Prayers

Unresolved trauma from our pasts create unmet needs, unhealed hurts, and unresolved issues deep within our souls. These needs, hurts, and issues become "sources" of fuel for feelings of pain, fear, distrust, hopelessness, anger, and wrong desires.

To survive the intense force of these negative attitudes and emotions, we all learn "behaviors" that enable us to cope with our feelings of vulnerability and doubt. When we do not know how to break out of these entrenched coping patterns, we try to justify and rationalize our inability to overcome them by building strongholds to defend them.

The key to overcoming every stage of this cycle of defeat and pain is to dismantle the core structure of our souls' power and control that has been blocking the healing work of the Holy Spirit. Then God's mercy and grace can get into our "sources" and heal them.

God will not violate your free will by forcing His way into your self-protected areas of pain in order to heal you. This full-color laminated diagram of these workings within the unsurrendered soul, as well as binding and loosing prayers on the back, will help you understand why even Christians can feel so undone sometimes.

Order the charts with MasterCard or Visa on a message/fax line (916-344-5111) or e-mail your order to liberty@calweb.com. All credit card orders require an additional $3.00 S&H charge per order.

Charts may also be ordered by mail with money order or personal check.

Allow three weeks for delivery. No additional S&H necessary with this choice of payment. You may also request a sample copy of the free quarterly teaching newsletter.

| Laminated Chart | (Full size) | (8.5" x 11") | $6.00 ea. |
| Laminated Chart | (Bible size) | (5" x 8") | $4.00 ea. |

Send orders to: Liberty Savard Ministries
P.O. Box 41260
Sacramento CA 95841